THE CONSCIOUS COMMUNICATOR

The Pursuit of Joy and Human Connection

Inspired by the Art of Horsemanship

NIKKI PORTER

BALBOA.
PRESS

A DIVISION OF HAY HOUSE

Balboa Press books may be ordered through booksellers or by contacting:

Balboa Press
A Division of Hay House
1663 Liberty Drive
Bloomington, IN 47403
www.balboapress.com
1 (877) 407-4847

Because of the dynamic nature of the Internet, any web addresses or links contained in this book may have changed since publication and may no longer be valid. The views expressed in this work are solely those of the author and do not necessarily reflect the views of the publisher, and the publisher hereby disclaims any responsibility for them.

The author of this book does not dispense medical advice or prescribe the use of any technique as a form of treatment for physical, emotional, or medical problems without the advice of a physician, either directly or indirectly. The intent of the author is only to offer information of a general nature to help you in your quest for emotional and spiritual well-being. In the event you use any of the information in this book for yourself, which is your constitutional right, the author and the publisher assume no responsibility for your actions.

Interior Image Credit: Stanley Walker

Print information available on the last page.

ISBN: 978-1-9822-1737-2 (sc)
ISBN: 978-1-9822-1735-8 (hc)
ISBN: 978-1-9822-1736-5 (e)

Library of Congress Control Number: 2018914276

Balboa Press rev. date: 12/14/2018

Dedicated to my daughter Blake.

Sweet Blake, never let your fears outweigh your dreams. I love you to the satellites.

CONTENTS

MY INTENTION

"Knowing how to think empowers you far beyond those who know only what to think."

Neil deGrasse Tyson

What if I told you that you could deliberately change how you communicate with yourself and everyone around you to create amazing relationships and a much happier you? Would you want in immediately? If so, perfect.

I began writing this book as a part of my personal journey to compile what I have learned and designed it to teach you how to take your thoughts off of autopilot and help you to become mindful in your communications. This book is for anyone who finds themselves feeling frustrated with a loved one, wanting to scream at a stranger in their car, or holding onto resentment.

It is my hope that this book teaches you new skills to bring you confidence you may have never experienced before, and will allow you a new level of control over your life. We are all capable of being happy. We are in the driver's seat of our own lives, but we may have to learn new ways to navigate the road to get us exactly where we want to be.

I have been privileged to own horses since a young age. As a result of building a relationship with horses, I was taught the importance of clear communication. As my horsemanship advanced, and my husband and I taught others how to communicate more effectively with their horses, I began to connect the dots. I realized everything I had learned about how to improve the relationship between horse and human could be applied to every type of relationship. As I started to use what I learned working with horses to the people around me, I saw two incredible shifts. The first shift was in myself. The more intentional I was in my communication with myself, the better my communication became with others, and the more control I felt over my life. I began to react with more reason and less emotion. I started to treat people more fairly. I began to make myself accountable for my happiness. The second shift I experienced was with my family and close friends, and eventually with all of my interactions. I was able to reflect on other's responses and react from a place of clear perspective rather than reactive judgment or hurt feelings.

There is no question improving the relationships in our lives, from romantic to business, removes a lot of daily stress. Without trust and respect, relationships are unstable, whether it be our relationship with ourselves or with others. We invest time and money to learn skills to help us achieve more in our jobs and sports. Rarely do we invest in ourselves and our relationships because we believe we are who we are and they are who they are. I was not content with this. I knew I still had room for growth. In all honesty, I don't believe I will ever stop evolving and neither will you. There is an endless amount of knowledge for us to learn about ourselves, the world around us, and how we live our lives. This book highlights some of the most important lessons I have been taught so far.

The concepts I will discuss are not new; I am certainly not the first to come up with them. However, it was through working with horses that their importance rang true for me. Without clear communication with my horses, things went wrong. I could see that I was holding our relationships back because they were not "getting" what I was teaching them. I had to become more conscious of my communication with my horse if I wanted to advance. This meant I had to take ownership of my actions and the response I would get from my horse. There is no room for blame when working with horses because everything they offer us is a result of what we are doing and communicating; they are simply responding.

As I began to want to better myself as a person, not just as a *horse person*, I discovered that my path to better horsemanship mirrored my path to becoming a better human. I had to become more conscious of my communication, first with myself and then with others. As working with horses taught me, I had to take ownership of my actions and the responses I was giving and getting in every situation. I found this also applied when I worked on my mindset. Everything offered to us is a result of what we are doing and communicating. The universe is merely responding.

I want it to be clear before we begin, I am not saying that we need to treat humans as we treat horses and vice versa. That will never work because we are so different. I do not want you to work with your family as if you are training a horse, so in this light, I will not be going into detail about the training methods used. Not only that but when we treat our horses like humans we get ourselves into various miscommunications with them. What I do want you to learn are the concepts we use when we teach our students how to work with their horses in a way that allows for better communication. These concepts teach us the importance of conscious communication. Communicating with humans and horses is not one and the same, although our ability to communicate from a place of clear intent and conscious effort is.

If you picked up this book because you thought it was meant to teach you how to train your horse, you are not entirely off base. It will help. However, my desire is for you to learn about yourself. If you do not own a horse and likely never will, this book is as much for you as the person who was born in a barn. You, my friend, are who I had in mind when I began writing because you deserve these lessons too, whether or not you had the opportunity or interest in owning horses. My use of horsemanship is what has tuned me into these life lessons. With every horse and rider I work with I learn more about them as people than I do as horse owners. I think this is where the magic is.

After applying these concepts to my own life, I began to read and research as much as I could about how to shift to conscious thought to intentionally create a happier life. Not only had I connected my knowledge of working with horses to how to communicate with people, but I had also connected my knowledge of mindfulness to empower myself. These aspects aligned seamlessly to help me recognize the control that I possess over my present and my future happiness.

I began to crave knowledge related to improving myself, and in doing so, I learned that it all comes down to connection through conscious communication. If I wanted a better relationship with my horse, I needed to learn how to create a better connection; be less mechanical and more present. If I wanted a better relationship with my family, I needed to learn to be less reactive and more empathetic—this applied to my horse as well. If I wanted a better relationship with myself, I needed to learn how to be less concerned about conforming and more conscious of what brings me joy. Interestingly, I can also apply that last part to my horses and husband. It all connects.

With almost every riding lesson I teach, the connection between why something is going wrong with my student's horse and how it relates to the rest of their life is made. I often hear my student say, "Oh you just described how I am with my husband," or I will see someone shoot their friend or partner a knowing look as I talk them through why their horse is responding the way they do to them. When we work with horses, they reflect who and what we are. If we are anxious they become anxious, if we are fearful they become fearful, and if we are calm, they become calm. All of these emotions influence our thoughts and inadvertently our responses. When we are frustrated with our horses, we react with anger and a lack of patience, just as we do when we become frustrated with another person.

Becoming conscious of our communication in all aspects of our life results in a lot more connection, and isn't connection what we all seek? We feel sad when we feel like we have no friends, we feel drained when our relationship is missing something, we feel depressed when we lose touch with ourselves, and we feel anxious when we feel like we are alone. Conscious communication fuels connection and connection fuels our souls.

According to scientist Matthew Lieberman's research, as humans, we are made for connection.[1] It has been argued that we need connection just as we need food and water. Our brains are wired to be social. Now in a world of social networking, we need to focus on creating quality connections more than ever before. One of the reasons I believe some people love working with horses, or any animal at that, is the connection they feel and the understanding they come to hold close. When someone builds a relationship with a horse through clear communication, the connection that exists is inspirational. If these majestic, powerful animals trust and respect us, they will look to us for guidance even when their instincts tell them to run. Connection with a horse makes us feel all of the things we desire in any relationship. It makes us feel loved, needed, listened to, trusted, and empowered. Tell me, who wouldn't want to work toward a relationship with their spouse, child, friend, or anyone else, that made them feel this way?

We have the ability to create connections with people the same way we create bonds with animals, though we will only be able to do it through mindful communication, verbal and nonverbal. This means we will likely not be able to maintain these connections solely through social media and texting, the technology which seems to drive non-connection.

It is critical we connect on a level that is beyond what is possible through technology. I think this is something that needs to be addressed as I believe we are all aware of the effects of cell phones and social media on our communication and relationships. With this in mind, when you read the word "communicate" written on these pages, understand that it is addressing communication beyond texting and emails. Here, a connection is the energy that surges between people, not devices.

My intention is when you set this book down you will feel empowered to consciously choose your thoughts, your words, and your actions. That you will awaken knowledge from within yourself that has always been there—and you will finally give yourself permission to embrace it. My hope is that you will transform your relationship with yourself and everyone you meet. Take time to complete the exercises presented to you at the end of each chapter to gain personal insight and track your growth.

Now is the time to put the work into the things that matter most: To treat your relationships with the care they deserve and to recognize that to shift your thinking can bring about a new sense of happiness.

FOUNDATION OF TRUST
AND RESPECT

"All bonds are built on trust, without it you have nothing."

Unknown

When interacting with horses, the most successful partnerships come from a foundation of trust and respect. I believe this is true with people as well. Trust and respect come from clear, authentic, and empathetic communication.

How we build relationships with people based on trust and respect is complex, and yet simple. There are many factors which help to establish trust and respect in every type of relationship we have, including intimate relationships, friendships, business partnerships, parent-child relationships. Clear and conscious communication is key to building and maintaining trust and respect in all of our relationships. In the chapters to follow, we will delve deeper into communication and empathy.

It is essential that we understand what happens in our relationships where trust exists. Trust means that you believe you can depend on someone, you have confidence in them, and you feel safe with them both emotionally and physically. Trust eliminates the fear of mistreatment, betrayal, and judgment. Trust also allows a space for vulnerability, honesty, and growth, which creates sustainable relationships and makes us happier people overall. Happiness, after all, is a skill that can be learned.

Studies have shown that people who consider themselves to be happy have genuine habits, and one of those includes paying attention to their relationships.[2] We must pay attention and create deliberate habits that prioritize and nourish our connections with others. Here is the kicker: Quality relationships with others also require us to have a quality relationship with ourselves. It is vital that we focus inward and recognize our self-talk. Without trust and respect for ourselves, we cannot truly build healthy relationships with others because we will have unclear intentions and doubt instead of communicating from a place of self-love and mindfulness. How we communicate with ourselves affects how we interact with others. When we treat our relationship with ourselves with as much trust and respect as we expect with others, we communicate from a whole new level of love and confidence.

While writing this book, I connected with a friend online who seemed to be in the same stage of growth as I was. She suggested I read a book by Brené Brown she thought I would love. While I read the book, I had revelation after revelation which brought so many emotions. I found myself nodding as her words seemed to be shaped around how I was feeling and what I needed to hear precisely at that moment.

Brené Brown, Ph.D., LMSW, breaks down the anatomy of trust in her book *Braving the Wilderness.* I was listening to the audiobook while I revised my manuscript and I found myself scrambling for a pen and paper to jot down Brown's acronym: *BRAVING*.[3] My mind flew to this chapter, and I knew what I had learned from *Braving the Wilderness* had to be added. Brown's book was life-changing for me. Below is her breakdown of the acronym, paraphrased. I highly suggest you read this work for yourself to gain all it has to offer.

B = Boundaries: Having my own and respecting yours.

R = Reliability: Being reliable and authentic (real).

A = Accountability: I take ownership of my mistakes, apologize and make amends.

V = Vault: I will not share what is not mine to share; no gossiping, respect confidentiality.

I = Integrity: Courage over comfort; practicing my values, not only professing them.

N = Non-judgment: Asking for what we need and feel without judgment.

G = Generosity: Believing the best of intentions from others; not victimizing myself.

Brown's acronym applies to trusting yourself and others. It is important to note we cannot expect from others what we do not give to ourselves. It is imperative that we learn to treat ourselves with the same expectations we place on others. When we do this our expectations come from a place of experience, understanding, and compassion. Brown truly said it best when she said, *"If you find yourself in struggle with trust, the thing to examine first: how you treat yourself."*[4]

Throughout this book we will be looking at individual practices to help us communicate clearly with ourselves and with those around us that aid in promoting, establishing, and maintaining a healthy relationship. Your confidence will soar with the ability to approach life from a place of inner power and control, rather than one of misplaced emotion and impulse.

Lower stress is another benefit to maintaining healthy relationships and interacting daily from a place of consciousness. The emotional chaos that results from stress can make our daily lives overwhelming and can negatively impact our physical health. Learning how to become more mindful in our interactions will help to alleviate stress that does not need to exist.

Stress is a biological and psychological response experienced when we encounter a threat which we feel we are unable to deal with; we need a level of stress to keep us alive. Crippling stress, however, is not limited to life-threatening situations. Often, we feel like we are unable to deal with a situation because our automatic thoughts, the first thoughts we have in that moment, tell us that is so. When we begin to change our unconscious thought to conscious thought, we begin to reduce stress because we approach situations logically rather than from a place of displaced anger, unhealthy internal dialog, or exaggerated emotional reaction. We are our own worst enemy when we become prisoners of our thoughts we perceive as always true. We need to challenge our learned and conditioned way of thinking and rise to a deliberate and meaningful thought process which allows us to live in a happier state of being.

The increased optimism, which comes from trusting and respecting ourselves and others, is empowering and contagious. Our new approach of intentional interaction with our own thoughts and the people around us will enhance our control of our lives in a way we perhaps have never experienced. We will feel less taken advantage of and more valued. We will feel less manipulated and more appreciated. When we become more optimistic, we create our lives rather than react to it because we are in control of our thoughts, our responses, and our decisions; we gain a new sense of power that others will notice. This new approach brings a feeling of lightness and freedom because there isn't the weight of unnecessary worry, resentment, and self-doubt.

The concepts discussed in this book all aid in conscious, clear, and empathetic communication to build trust and respect and allow healthy relationships to develop and flourish.

Mindfulness

As important as it is that I explain common terms such as trust and respect, I also want to clarify what I mean when I use the words "mindfulness" and "mindful" in this book. As a reader, I'd like you to understand these terms reference a conscious awareness that we can include in our daily lives when we interact with others for pleasure and business. Therefore, I am not referring to the practice of meditation, although I highly recommend you learn the meditative skill because it can also bring you closer in your quest for a mindful and happier life.

In this book, mindfulness, as I refer to it, is being able to see situations and life more clearly. Mindfulness is being present in each moment. A great mantra I have heard and have used is, *"Be here now."* I first heard this while in a workshop on mindfulness put on by Cindy O'Donnell, hosted at her spa Kini Wellness. I was drawn to this particular event because it was being hosted at a spa that included "float pods" and I was very curious about what the concept of floating would be like. Through my curiosity about practice of floating, I attended her mindfulness workshop with my sister. It was perfect timing for me because throughout the event Cindy spoke about so many things that I had been learning in the months prior.

The mantra Cindy used connected my *want* to practice mindfulness daily to the actualization of it. If you have not heard of what a mantra is exactly, it is a word or phrase which is repeated. Repeating a mantra is a great way to begin controlling our thoughts, rather than our thoughts controlling us. Repeating *"Be here now"* shifts our consciousness to the present moment and helps us to be more mindful. One of the best definitions of mindfulness, in tune with how I use it in this book, is this:

> *Mindfulness creates a space, a pause in which you can respond considerately to situations, rather than react. The new breakthroughs in neuroscience show that by practicing mindfulness, the brain can be shaped for greater happiness, love, wisdom and greater emotional balance in turbulent times, as well as healthier relationships, more effective actions, and greater peace of mind.*[5]

I like this definition of mindfulness because the term "mindfulness" evokes a meaning which it actually is not. "Mind-*ful*-ness" makes us think our mind should be full. However, it should be the opposite. Mindfulness offers space in our minds by taking control of the continuous, non-productive thoughts which ramble on and prevent us from responding consciously and effectively. As you read this book, I will repeatedly emphasize the importance of mindfulness in the use of clear communication. To be mindful in communication with horses and humans, you must listen and speak with kindness, compassion, and awareness.

Mindful communication takes practice and demands a level of self-awareness. Words hold so much power, and when we use them carefully and deliberately we have the ability to positively affect our own lives and the lives of many others.

To truly be successful using the concepts outlined in this book, it is helpful to offer tips to help guide our thoughts toward more mindful communication. These are the tips to inform the practices which will help us become more successful as we create and maintain the best relationships possible with those we love:

1. Listen to Hear: Approach conversations with an open mind and listen to hear rather than to respond. Do not try to manipulate a conversation to go in a specific direction. Allow your response to be dictated by what the other person says, not in the direction you would like it to go. A great way of doing this is trying to take "I" out of your responses. If you listen to hear the other person, you have a better chance of responding with empathy and compassion and will begin to relate to them as "we" versus "I." This approach is what prompted me to write this book from the perspective I have. I use "I" and "you" when needed, however, I stick to "we" as much as possible. I am not pointing my finger at you as a reader and saying *you* must change or *you* must become more mindful. I am saying "we" because mindfulness is a skill and every suggestion that I pass along to you, I also have to practice daily to maintain. Another skill to practice is to listen without thinking: Do not think of your response while the person you are listening to is speaking. Simply listen to learn. It is very similar to listening to an audiobook or professor offering a lecture. When we listen to learn and not to respond, we reflect after we hear the information and do not try to impose our own opinions or sway the speaker to another direction.

2. Speak Softly: By softly I do not necessarily mean with the quiet tone of our voice, yet that can be a factor. The first chapter delves deeply into the concept of softness. Nevertheless, as a pre-emptive note, being soft is being mindful of how we speak to others. We do not speak to win; we speak from a place of thought and truth.

3. Be Present: Being present means we are able to be mindful in our response to situations. We do not let negative personal experiences or feelings get in the way of our understanding. We are rational in our response and communicate with an open and honest heart and mind. Working with horses has taught me the importance of presence; horses never think of the future, they respond in the moment only. We, as human beings, live in a world that lacks presence. We praise multitasking and working today for the future we want tomorrow, rather than building a happy life today, one that will result in a happy future.

We must be careful not to put pressure on ourselves to set a goal to be perfectly mindful at all times, starting now. If we set such a lofty goal, we will set ourselves up for failure. And because of an unrealistic goal, we can count on us feeling less happy, and quite disappointed in ourselves. We are embarking on a journey to create new habits in our communication that will lead to a happier life. Let's set ourselves up for success rather than failure.

Start small and remember consistency is key to creating new habits. If we decide that as of now we are to be mindful every minute of every day, we will not build confidence. Instead, let's take it one interaction at a time: One conversation, one flip-off by a stranger, one confused look from our spouse, at a time. We should take the time to notice our thoughts throughout our day and practice non-thought. When we are free of thinking is when we will find the space to pause, and little by little we will claim our control and happiness.

We will set small goals and throughout this book be encouraged to complete mindful exercises that offer insight and reflection on ourselves and our relationships.

Intention

We cannot discuss mindfulness without also touching on intention. I have come to believe that intention is one of the biggest contributing factors in our success with everything we do. This book shows how our intentions affect our communication. As with the other concepts I share and explain in this book, the awareness of how intention affects the connection between horse and human came before I ever applied it to relationships with people. The fact that horses communicate and understand a great deal through body language beyond what humans can likely fathom shows its importance.

I was listening to Oprah's *Super Soul Sunday* podcast one day while cleaning the barn and I had a breakthrough moment. She was explaining, along with the help of other incredible forward thinkers, the importance of intention. I thought, *Yes! This is why so many people I work with are having so much trouble communicating with their horses!*

I took a moment to think and clarify what I had just realized, and from that point on I tried to apply it to my own life and the people around me—with each success the true importance of intention became more apparent to me.

When I work with other people's horses, I often bring them into a round pen. This is a smaller pen, commonly 50 feet in diameter. I allow the horse to be loose with me in the pen and I start by adding soft pressure to have the horse look to me, and through that I begin to create a connection. Quite often I have found horses who hide. They seem to shut their eyes to my pressure and body language. They will sometimes respond by stopping their feet, resulting in the horse standing still by the rail with their head turned away from me, or by running by me—another way to ignore me. I always find this interesting because I am not teaching them something new in the round pen, I am simply using body language to communicate that they can trust me. What I find most intriguing is that they have stopped trusting their own instincts so much that it becomes a learning process for them to see that my pressure and release matches what they think my intentions are.

Horses who are handled by people whose pressure and release do not match their intentions become defensive, confused, and frustrated. For clarification, pressure and release refers to when we ask for something and then stop asking. For example, when I'm riding I ask my horse to go forward by squeezing with my legs, I stop squeezing when my horse does what I have asked for. The release communicates that they have responded correctly. Oftentimes, riders will confuse horses by not releasing their pressure at the right time, or sometimes not at all. Horses treated this way stop trusting their incredible gift of reading the subtlest body language and resort to answers they have learned might take the pressure off instead; like ignoring their handler, overreacting, or acting aggressively. They do this because when they trusted their instinct in the past and responded to the body language of the handler, the pressure and release did not match the perceived intention and they were punished as a result.

An example of this would be someone asking their horse to simply go faster, the horse responds appropriately to the pressure and quickens their pace. The rider, who may be a bit green or new, then grabs the reins and pulls the horse to a stop. Unfortunately, their release to the horse happens as the horse stiffens, throws its head in the air, and slams its feet into the ground in a very uncomfortable stop, teaching the horse to brace and stop poorly in the future.

Another scenario I have seen is a rider who asks their horse to do something without being present enough or aware enough to acknowledge the horse's effort to find the correct answer. As a result, the ask and the rewarded answer do not match. This happens most often when the person who is handling the horse is unclear on their intention; they settle for the responses the horse offers because they are nervous or unsure, and their pressure either quits too soon or never quits.

For our communication to be clear and for others to truly trust us, our actions, words, and intentions have to match and be consistent. When others perceive our intentions as one thing, yet we do things to contradict those intentions, trust is impossible. Just as horses learn not to trust the intentions of their human due to confusing communication, humans are just as easily defeated. I think this is something we all need to work on. If we do not know our intentions 100% or the intentions others believe we have, our actions and words may not match. This is a fast track for miscommunication which creates problems in our relationships.

When we enter into relationships of all kinds, we should know our intentions and be sure that our actions and words communicate those intentions clearly. If we meet someone and we intend to form a non-romantic relationship with this person, our actions must match our intention for this person to trust us. I see young people in relationships who are confused by the status of their relationship because their partner's actions and words conflict with what the other person believes their intentions are. I hear stories of girls and guys who get their hearts broken because they learn that the person they were pouring their time, energy, and feelings into had no intention of a serious relationship. And yet their words, actions, and body language up to that point communicated they did. These conflicting experiences—along with many others—create doubt and mistrust. Clear communication is also fair communication. It is not fair to intend one thing and communicate something else.

Respect tends to follow trust. It is when we can trust that someone is true to their word and that they mean what they say that they are worthy of our admiration, trust, and our respect. Both trust and respect are difficult to achieve or maintain when we send mixed signals.

The key to clear communication is being mindful of our intentions when we interact with others, human or animal, and be true to them in how we communicate. In order for us to know what we intend we should take time to think and feel so we can be clear on what we truly aim for. Our intentions get picked up on through our body language and our energy. We can communicate this clearly by being present in our bodies and responding in the moment rather than responding based on past experiences, current fears, or hopes for the future.

CHAPTER ONE

BE SOFT

*"Just because you are soft doesn't mean that you are not
a force. Honey and wildfire are both the color gold."*

Victoria Erickson

In the horse world, we have a term to describe someone who
is soft. We say they have "feel." Feel is something that the best
horsemen possess. It is the very thing that allows a human to
achieve incredible things with their equine partner while looking
like they are doing nothing at all. When I began teaching others
to ride I was unsure if "feel" was something I could teach. I tried
many tricks to relay the concept to riders who did not seem to
possess it naturally. I would give vocal cues that told them when

they were feeling the desired effect. I would try holding the other end of their reins in my hands in hopes to demonstrate that skill through direct teaching. It was not until I truly understood how the concept applied to life and people as a whole that I discovered how to teach it with horses successfully.

I was on social media one day, and someone shared a post that stopped me in my tracks. It simply stated: *"You approached it like it was heavy, so it was."* -Unknown author.[6]

I let that sink in. I took a moment to read it again. *"You approached it like it was heavy, so it was."* This was my epiphany moment. After reading it a few times and not quite understanding why it hit me so hard, I realized it was the exact clarification I had been looking for. It provided the understanding and the answer for why some riders do not grasp the concept of softness, and was why some people struggle to see the greatness and the light in their lives.

When we approach something, anything, with the expectation that it will be difficult, impossible, draining, resistant, or damaging, it *will* be. When we expect the worst, we do not approach the situation with softness; we approach it with an edge that results in the very thing we wish to avoid.

When I attended a horsemanship clinic with the incredible horseman Jim Anderson of Alberta, Canada, he said that when handling horses, peoples' initial ask is often too heavy or hard.[7] When they do not get the desired response to what they are asking, they do not continue to build pressure to communicate clearly what is being asked. This results in them never getting the horse to do exactly what they believe they are asking for. When I thought of how this relates to our communication with other people, I was reminded that words and tones can feel like a physical push to humans. I think the most crucial lesson that needs to be drawn from this is when applying it to people is the initial ask. Later I will visit the problems that occur in relationships due to unclear or ambiguous "gray" communication, rather than clear black and white.

People respond to softness in the same way horses do. When we approach someone with a softer tone, softer body language, or a soft touch even, they tend to trust us easier. During the times when we do slip, and handle a situation harsher than necessary, it is easier for friends and family to forgive because they will be on less of a defense with us. Softness creates trust, and then we feel comfortable opening up, being ourselves—or making mistakes—because we know that the reaction is going to suit the trusting relationship we have built with the other person as well as the situation. Interacting with softness takes personal awareness. Horsemen and women pay professionals to teach them how to build this awareness with their animal, yet we do not often apply the same awareness or take the same care with our human interactions and relationships. We should be spending the same amount of time, thought, and money investing in ourselves to benefit our relationships with others as we do with our animals and other passions, such as sports. When we invest in ourselves, we incidentally invest in our relationships as well, horse and human alike.

To explain the importance of mindfulness to achieve softness in communication, I will use an analogy of crime and punishment. When we do not consciously interact with softness, we risk overreacting to situations. Rather than our initial *ask* being too heavy, or strong, our *reaction* is too harsh, quick, or hard, which is just as detrimental. I often see this with children, and being a mom myself, I recognize this one is tough but so important.

Let's use the example of a busy toddler and a tired mom. This situation rings true to my heart because it is one I find I have had to consciously work through the most over the last couple years.

The child reaches for something and mistakenly knocks over a glass of milk. The little one did not spill their milk intentionally, and their reaction and memory of their mistake will significantly depend on the reaction of their mother or regular caretaker when mistakes are made. Here are two scenarios of how this situation could play out:

Response Option #1

As the drained mom sees the spilled milk, she responds harshly. She allows her inner voice to take control of the situation and she communicates in frustration, anger, and disappointment through a raised voice, quick and hasty movements, and an angered expression. Without seeing the teachable moment consciously, the mother is, in fact, teaching her child other important lessons with her knee-jerk and overactive response: "Mistakes are unacceptable," "You are bad," "You cannot look to me for understanding," and even "You are stupid." These are not phrases that play through the young mind of a toddler. They are messages sent to the subconscious that get reinforced with every situation where an adult does not appropriately control their emotional response toward others, such as their children. This response also does not fit the crime and shows the importance of self-awareness and being mindful in our interactions with others, especially impressionable children.

As a mom, I know this is hard to read and accept. Please understand that if you are becoming defensive as you read this, you are not alone and your response is understandable. Your reaction likely comes from the same place of automatic and unconscious thought I have just referred to. I need you to understand that I am not cautioning the mom who occasionally slips up and allows her emotions to boil over. We all get to this point sometimes, no matter how in tune we are with ourselves. I am cautioning those who consistently handle their children in this manner.

Not only does this kind of unconscious response to our children contribute to a negative inner voice for the child, but it also teaches them that it is okay to respond emotionally rather than rationally.

When children are consistently handled in emotionally charged, harsh, or negative ways, they will internalize it. It reinforces that we do not need to handle others with empathy, kindness, and love; that it is okay to treat others aggressively and inappropriately and yet still expect them to love, trust, and respect us. Later in life, as a young adult and in adulthood, they may have this message return to them as they navigate through their relationships. I foresee two possible outcomes of how this may play out in their future are these:

1: We will see them enter into relationships where they accept emotional and physical abuse because they will believe that is what they are worthy of and those harsh emotional reactions are normal and healthy or:

2: They will become the aggressor. They will not see the importance of monitoring and self-regulating their emotional responses to others, responding to loved ones without sensitivity and compassion, and will still expect them to love, respect, and trust them.

Response Option #2

As the drained mom sees the spilled milk she responds softly and mindfully. To react softly in this situation, one must be present and overpower the potential knee-jerk reaction of frustration. We must be aware that this frustration comes from the inner voice that we often listen to without a second thought because that is what we have always done. It does not have to be so. With mindfulness, we can intentionally change our inner dialog and shift to become more conscious communicators.

In a moment, the mom responds consciously and manages to have the punishment fit the crime. She does not raise her voice. She does not become rigid. She acknowledges that it is a teaching moment and has the appropriate conversation about taking our time and the importance of helping clean up our messes. Also, she addresses that we all make mistakes and it is "no big deal" even though her internal dialog initially told her it *was* a big deal. She is exhausted and believes she cannot take on one more task. She can, and she does because her happiness and her child's happiness depend on it.

The reaction of the child to this response will vary of course. Nonetheless having been met with softness and understanding, they begin to learn the range of appropriate emotional responses to different situations in life. An appropriate emotional response is an essential learned skill for children. If we respond consciously as a parent, we will teach them to begin to do the same. They must understand that they will receive a different response based on different situations. If we respond to spilled milk the same way we react to them stepping out into traffic we will teach them that any situation that creates an emotional response in them is one that they should react quickly, assertively, or hastily to.

Another outcome worth briefly discussing is the internal dialog this sort of lack of softness or lack of an appropriate emotional response creates. A child who is always scolded for their mistakes rather than guided and educated through understanding will fear making mistakes. In turn, they might limit the risks they take, small and large, as a means to lessen the expected ridicule, judgment, or harsh reactions of those around them. Potentially they could suffer from anxiety, negative self-talk, engage in self-harm, and be prone to commit to unhealthy relationships. That being said, our experiences do not shape us entirely.

It must be recognized that an individual's innate characteristics may be as or more influential than their past experiences. We as parents must not count on that. The great thing about this is it can be changed through personal or professional help. Those individuals can learn about presence and a way of thinking that will help them break free from conforming to unconscious thought patterns, unhealthy emotional responses, and limiting self-beliefs.

I need to be clear here; I am not calling out all parents who have acted harshly in times of frustration or exhaustion or habit. I wrote this to bring awareness and to show the real importance of approaching others with softness and personal knowledge. It is difficult to react perfectly every time, and if you can, I would like to shake your hand.

I believe that none of us are perfect. One day while writing this book I told my daughter I was going to drop her off on the side of the highway because she would *not* stop kicking the back of my seat while I was driving. You know what I'm talking about here. I wasn't serious when I said it and she laughed and said I would never do that. We laughed together, but if I were being assessed by the conscious communication police, I would have been taken in for questioning or at least given a warning. Had my child, however, started to cry at that moment and begged me not to stop the car, I would have had to do some major questioning of myself and why she took me seriously or became upset. How others respond to us gives us the perfect opportunity to assess our personal communication. A five-year-old may not *always* give you a perfect assessment, but I think a child's reactions tend to tell us more than we may want to admit sometimes.

I encourage you to become conscious of when and how you react and whether it was based on a negative internal dialog; one which caused you to disconnect from the true nature and gravity of the situation. If you read this and it makes you reflect on yourself, then it is a win. If it allows you to change your response through conscious thought one out of ten times, then that is also a win.

Growth happens in small steps, and the most essential part of growth is the acknowledgment of who we are now and who we want to become. We must acknowledge our weaknesses in order to work toward being a better version of ourselves. Do not be surprised if this new awareness brings a level of emotion.

Through my work with horses, I have discovered that growth

and change look a lot like vulnerability and we have likely been told in the past that this is a weakness. Do not be fooled; this is a show of strength like no other. We need to allow ourselves to feel vulnerable, but we must be careful here to not get stuck on our vulnerability and dwell in shame. We are not alone in how we act and feel. When we feel emotion as a result of growth, we need to observe the feeling while it is happening and accept that it needs to flow through us to exit; feel it leave and be thankful to be aware of the experience enough that there is no judgment attached. We are not weak, wrong, or broken for feeling vulnerable; we use it as a motivator to become who we truly want to be.

In an online course I took led by Eckhart Tolle he discussed "presence." He explained the ability to reach a new level of consciousness through the awareness and control over unconscious self-talk. Later I found a powerful quote where he said, *"Rather than being your thoughts and emotions, be the awareness behind them."*[8] Here Eckhart Tolle encouraged me and gave me permission to question my own thoughts and become someone stronger and more perceptive, should I choose. I suggest reading his material if you have not done so already. We cannot truly approach things differently unless we have a level of self-awareness. The key is to learn to manage our own self-talk. With this, we will no longer approach life on autopilot, where we react to things unconsciously and with thoughts that create negative ripples in our lives. A commonly accepted belief is that it takes 21 days to change or create a habit. I go further and suggest it takes more than time. It takes self-awareness and time. Be patient with yourself; it all starts with self-awareness.

Let's connect back to the idea of the skilled horseman because it is an incredible metaphor for our relationships with others. I'll refer to the term "feel" again. At the beginning of this chapter, I discussed how riders or handlers who are "soft" have what's called "good feel." So how do we approach people with softness?

Feel, when interacting with humans, would refer to our ability to communicate with others in a way that is most appropriate for the situation. People with the best feel seem to be able to read others' energy and the situation at hand and adjust themselves accordingly. These individuals tend to get into fewer unnecessary disputes, and they are the ones we find comforting and compassionate, yet motivating.

Sometimes, however, the motivators in our lives are not always speaking in soft tones. They are not always holding our hand and giving us chocolate for comfort. They may do these things when necessary, but they recognize and pull back when those actions are enabling us to wallow in self-doubt, create excuses that hold us back, deflect our guilt or pain on others, and dim our own light.

My husband and I remind the riders and handlers we teach that it is important to be *"Gentle in what we do, but firm in how we do it."*[9] This is a well-known line spoken by a horseman, Buck Brannaman. People with "feel" know when to push and when to comfort, the same as the advanced horseman who knows the appropriate amount of pressure to apply, when to apply specific types of pressure, and when to release pressure. Skilled horsemen also know when to show love and when to show leadership in other ways. A horseman who increases their pressure to communicate clearly with their horse can still be considered soft. The term soft comes from our initial and most appropriate approach in a given situation. Soft does not mean we are never straightforward and to the point. It means we do not enter into a situation responding at a higher degree of pressure or emotion than is necessary. It means that we have feel and can gain respect through conscious action that builds a relationship of mutual trust and understanding.

When we are not aware of our approach with others and do not interact mindfully, we are likely to speak too harsh unintentionally. We tend to speak with a tone that confuses the situation or show signs of irritation in our facial expressions and other non-verbal communication cues that make the other person uneasy. They might even question what they had done to annoy us when that wasn't the case at all. Quite often there's a simple fix when you sense something's off: "Did I say something wrong?" or "What's wrong?" will suffice to snap us back into deliberate communication and will leave us apologizing for the miscommunication. Or will, sadly, open an unintended dialog that results in an out-of-the-blue confrontation. Mindful communication will remove unnecessary stress and create harmony in our relationships.

When I think of softness, I think of our ability to be vulnerable, yet strong. I find this comes more naturally with horses for me than in my personal life. And it's a two-way street: My struggle to achieve softness with people allows me to understand when someone struggles to achieve it with their horse.

Once again, to be soft with a horse, we say we have to have feel. When we take away the word "have" we are left saying "to be soft, we need to feel." This is significant in horsemanship and our human relationships. To interact with someone with genuine, empathetic responses, we absolutely must feel, and that means we are left in a pretty vulnerable position. To *feel* we must *trust*. I have discussed the need to have others trust us, but have yet to touch on our need to trust others.

When we lack trust, we lack softness because we are too scared to let our guard down to truly feel for fear we will get hurt. I have seen this with people and their horses, where they handle their horse defensively rather than softly. Once upon a time something happened while they were riding or working with horses, they were vulnerable, and it scared them. With each interaction, their goal, conscious or unconscious, is never to let that happen again. As a result, they handle the horse they had in the past and never have the opportunity to handle the horse in the present. We cannot achieve softness in this way.

As I just admitted, what I excel at with my horses, I have found challenging with people. Particularly, my husband. I struggle to soften my communication with him and have done a fair amount of reading on how to balance my feminine and masculine energy as a result of feeling "broken" at times. I would look at other women and wish I had their ability to be quiet, sweet, and fun. I get tired of being vocal, rational and, well, not fun! I used to show the movie *The Help* to my senior high English students and always felt envious of the character of Celia Foote because of the characteristics she possessed that I believe I lack. I wish I had even an ounce of her bubbly, feminine, unassuming nature.

I have come to the conclusion that I will never be bubbly and bouncy, yet I have the ability to be fun in my own reason-seeking ways. And by being mindful, I can be a softer version of myself. I have to continue to invest in knowing myself and communicate consciously from my genuine self, not the person that results from my need to *do* rather than *be*. When I slip up—which I do more often than I like—I do my best to apologize. Sometimes it takes me a matter of minutes to become self-aware of my reaction to a situation, and sometimes it hits me days later, either way, I try to address it.

Accountability is key to awareness. It does us no good to think *Damn, I am totally responsible for that mess of a conversation, I'll do better next time . . .* That intention is great but does nothing for the relationship at the time. Vocalizing that we acknowledge our behaviors and mistakes is what keeps us accountable in the future.

After spending a lot of time thinking about how I feel in situations, why I feel it, and how it manifests in my communication with my husband, I have come to a few conclusions.

I believe that I struggle to soften in my relationship with my husband as a result of a number of things. Now I am not blaming anyone for anything here. Our experiences simply mold us, and my experiences have had an impact on my ability to truly soften in my relationships.

I have a strong and independent mother who did an incredible job of teaching me how men should treat me and what not to accept, ever. She taught me how to have a backbone; how to voice my opinion and stick up for what I believe in. I am so thankful for that. I learned from her lessons that allowed me to be confident and to speak up for myself when boys stepped out of line when I was a young adult or treated me in ways I did not feel were right.

My mother's lessons truly saved me from some pretty awful situations and relationships in the past. I carried these lessons into my marriage. They have allowed me to set boundaries and communicate what I need. Despite this at times, I allow myself to get stuck being too assertive and have a difficult time just being soft and vulnerable.

I believe that my difficulty to feel vulnerable with my husband came from one relationship in particular in my past. When this relationship ended I said once, if not a hundred times: "I will never allow someone to make me feel that way again." In that relationship, I wore my heart on my sleeve. I was all feeling and no defense; he controlled my every emotion, and in the end, I was very hurt. Not only was I damaged by the end, I was taught a pretty powerful lesson, or so I thought: *When you are soft and vulnerable with a man, you will get hurt.*

I am now a married woman, and I still struggle to let my guard down and communicate from my heart rather than my head. My husband is loyal, loving, and affectionate and I will die working on my ability to soften for him. I trust him with my whole heart, and I see how much he loves me when he looks at me. And yet I still struggle.

I think it is important to note that my personality type and natural communication style influence my ability to be soft as well. I like to have control over my environment, and I am someone who would rather do something myself than delegate because then I know it is done and done the way I want it to be. I think my need for control likely contributes to my discomfort with softening, feeling, and letting go.

I know how important it is in my relationship with my husband to go against my instinct to protect myself. I know, much like a previously trampled horse owner, that if I approach my husband defensively, with the past controlling my present, our relationship will never reach its truest potential. In all reality, if I continue to defend myself, I may destroy our relationship altogether.

My love for my husband and our relationship has to overpower my want to protect myself from the emotional pain I have experienced in the past. I must allow myself to feel and trust as deeply as possible for him to be able to feel and trust in return. Just like our relationships with horses, the better our feel and the softer we become with one another, the closer to our potential we can reach. This is immeasurable.

I want to point out here that my relationship right now with my husband is wonderful and is the best, healthiest, and the most balanced relationship I have been in. Its development is comparable to the growth in my horsemanship. That being said, our relationship will go through ups and downs the same as every relationship. Knowing what we are when we are fantastic and deciding consciously to communicate the best we can when we are not is a big step to keeping our marriage alive.

In the past, I was successful with horses. I was very competitive and met all the goals I set out to do. I successfully competed in multiple disciplines, I broke and trained young ponies, and I won many championships. I don't mean this in a bragging way. More so that I had drive, resilience, and passion. I set my goals, and I worked and sacrificed to achieve them. I am proud of my accomplishments in my early years of working with horses. However, if anyone had told me in the past that my relationships with my horses were only brushing the surface of their potential, I would have thought they were crazy. Now that I am on the other side of growth, I am able to see how. I have become a much better communicator with my horse, and it has brought us to another level. I believe the same can and is happening with my marriage. The better we get at genuinely communicating and working with each other in ways we both need, understand, and appreciate, the better our relationship will be.

Be Consistent

Consistency is vital when working with horses. If we are unpredictable, we are not considered trustworthy. This applies to all relationships, horses and humans alike. As with horses, we need to treat people with consistent responses. We must remain true to our values to be consistent, and we have to hold ourselves and others to our boundaries in order to communicate clearly.

Consistency comes from self-awareness and self-control. We cannot be consistent in our words and actions if we are not aware of what we're trying to accomplish in the first place. We cannot allow ourselves to run on autopilot and slip into a reactive mental state where we overreact and underreact because being on autopilot places our power in the hands of others.

We not only have to be conscious of being consistent in our responding words and actions, but it is vital that we remain consistent in our efforts. We will all slip back into old habits, but if we are mindful, we will bounce back and work toward being more consistent in our communication with others.

As we bring our awareness consistently to our efforts, we will slip up less often, and more often we will catch ourselves and adjust or change our conditioned response; replacing words and actions we want to say from a place of frustration, blame, and hurt with words from a place of knowledge, empathy, and compassion.

Exercise:

This exercise is one that will promote mindfulness instead of our unchecked self-talk that can result in emotional responses we aren't so proud of. To soften our approach to self-talk, it is crucial that we recognize our typical responses when we become frustrated.

While having a conversation with Danique Henderson, a beautifully self-aware friend and fellow horsewoman, I experienced an aha moment that lead to an understanding of how the word "just" affects my communication with others. This insight created a shift and allowed me to take further control of my inner dialog and outward emotional responses toward others.

Danique pushed me to become more conscious of my inner dialog by exposing the use of the word "just." We have a tendency to use this word when we are frustrated with someone in a specific situation. We may say it in our head, or we may vocalize it. Notice when you say it now, become aware of when and why you are saying it.

By becoming more aware of when we use this word in frustration, we can begin to change our inner dialog and our emotions. When we shed light on the use of "just" within this specific context, it allows us mental space to pause and question the quality of the communication or lack thereof surrounding the situation. With this new understanding, and if we apply it to improved communication, we will change situations that otherwise would have left us with a multitude of negative emotions. We can flip them to situations that allow us to maintain a feeling of happiness, control, and contentment.

What to do:

Take note of the next time you are in a situation that makes you frustrated with a person or animal and their inability to meet your expectations in some way. Perhaps you find yourself saying, "Why can't they *just* put the dishes away?" or "Why don't they *just* stop treating me like a child?" or "Can't they *just* make the bed/put their socks in the hamper/take initiative?" The list goes on, and I bet it sounds familiar. Recognize the feeling of frustration in the speaker. Take a moment to acknowledge it and accept the emotion. You are not wrong to feel it, but you can take steps to create a happier mindset and change your reality by communicating in an appropriate way. The frustration you feel in that moment might be an indicator that your communication won't be quite as clear as you believe and considering this will give you the opportunity to change your approach.

When you recognize this happening, set aside some time that night with a journal. The process of writing is therapeutic and allows us to go back and revisit and contemplate our thoughts and words and interactions after the events take place. We may even begin to see a pattern of who we are becoming most frustrated with. We may recognize situations which bring about negative self-talk that influences your interactions with others. We may see that we are setting expectations for certain individuals or situations and never communicating those expectations. This will be discussed further in the next chapter.

In your journal write down a brief description of the situation, who was involved, and what you were doing. Next, think of how you were feeling at the time and let that resonate. What is it that you *just* wish the other person (or horse) would have done in that situation?

Now write out all the reasons why you wish they would have *just* done what you expected. Your reason may be: "to ease my stress," "to make me feel more appreciated," "to accomplish something more efficiently," "to save time," or, as often is the case with horses: "to show me they understood what I asked of them."

It is now time to delve into this deeper. Answer the following questions as honestly as possible:

Look back on a recent conflict in your life and ask yourself these questions:

1. Did I communicate my expectations clearly before the conflict occurred?
2. Did they intentionally frustrate me?
3. Why did they do what they did?
4. How could I have changed my communication to make my expectations clearer early on?
5. Is this a recurring situation? If yes, what have I done to improve the communication? If no, what could I have done to prevent the situation?

Now accept that it happened. Forgive yourself and the other individual.

Here is a little story you may be able to relate to:

A newly-married couple was doing barn chores after a hectic day and she, Franny, did something that frustrated her husband, Brad. Franny was a little distracted in her own head and did a task out of order and made her job less efficient than it could have been. It was not intentional on her part at all. Despite this, Brad saw her actions as a reflection of a lack of care or interest. He said the words, "Why didn't you *just* ask if you didn't know how to help?"

This took her back. The only response she could come up with was, "Because I *just* didn't." Franny had not considered what he expected her to do because she was not in the present moment, she was caught up thinking about an argument she had with her sister on the phone that morning. The argument had triggered an emotion in her earlier that day, and she was having a hard time letting it go. The communication on both of their parts had not been clear and his frustration with her was not going to change the past. His frustration in the moment was created by an unmet expectation. Vocalizing that frustration was not going to change the situation at hand. Besides, his reaction was not likely to make her change her behavior in the future because his response made her resentful and upset. She got defensive, and their communication did not improve the situation. It got worse, and they both left feeling unhappy and quiet.

This situation could resolve in a number of ways that would make moving on beyond the situation difficult or drawn out. The small situation could go without resolution altogether and be stored in one or both of their minds as ammunition for a future fight. However, if the couple had the intention to improve their relationship by becoming more conscious of their interactions, they would both have to reflect on and then discuss what took place in the barn. Moving beyond the miscommunication is made easy for this couple because they were able to communicate about the situation after it occurred.

Remember we must be patient with ourselves. In time we will discover this is how we begin our shift from communicating in a knee-jerk, unconscious manner to communicating consciously. We may still engage in unnecessary conflict, yet as we progress, we will be able to take responsibility for miscommunication rather than maintain a defensive and blame-deflecting stance. We will take the time to apologize. Before we know it, we will begin to control our thoughts in the moment more often and change our communication to leave a previously frustrating situation happy.

How might it have gone if Franny's husband acknowledged his frustration before speaking? Like this:

"Hunny, I think you misunderstood what I needed to have done. Maybe I wasn't clear. It would be more efficient if you did it this way so we can get done faster, and you can take me out for that nice birthday dinner you were planning. Sorry if I wasn't clear."

Franny may have responded with, "I'm sorry, I'm just a little fried from the day! Let's just get done and enjoy the rest of the night. What can I do next to help?"

End of conversation. No feelings of frustration, resentment, and annoyance on his part and no feelings of being judged, blamed, or hurt on her part. And the best part would be, the next time they did chores together, in light of the situation that occurred and without the cloud of negative feelings robbing Franny of the lesson to be learned, she would likely ask what needed to be done, rather than assume she knew and created more work for the both of them. Remember, problems aren't solved when they are wrapped in anger.

CHAPTER TWO
Release Pressure and Reward Good Behavior

*"Releasing the pressure, it's good for the
teapot and the water. Try it sometime."*

Jeb Dickerson

Rewarding good behavior is a concept that is generally accepted. We all know that positive reinforcement works for people and animals, and it is the conscious use of positive talk that creates shifts in relationships. With horses, the "talk" is the use of pressure and release and we, my husband and I, believe in the importance of "loving on them." When a horse responds correctly to pressure and the handler or rider releases that pressure immediately upon the desired result, that is where the horse learns. Once the horse has had the opportunity to process what just occurred, we believe showing them love will reinforce the positive response in order to maintain a relationship founded on trust and respect. Love can be demonstrated in several ways: It can be a break from work with no physical contact, or it could be through soft pats or a positive tone.

I have had the opportunity to learn from a horse which did not find comfort or reward in physical touch. As a handler, I found it difficult not to pat him when I was pleased with him. It was important for me to know that his release and reward was not the same as the majority of horses I had worked. When I discovered what worked, I ensured that he was rewarded in a way he enjoyed. As with people, horses respond as a result of past experiences. I was told that he likely had people trying to make him love them through physical touch, not realizing he did not like the pressure put on him.

This is an excellent lesson for building positive relationships with people as well. Humans respond to vocal and physical reward, but we do not all need or want the same. Some people are highly sensitive and quite shy. An exuberant and loud, "Well done!" with a big hug or high-five, even from someone they are very comfortable with, would make them uneasy. An appreciated reward for this type of person may have been a subtle nod and whisper of "I knew you could do it."

When we become more present with people, we begin to see the kind of interactions they enjoy, what they respond best to, and the appreciated way to encourage them. Usually, you can tell how someone likes interacting with people by how they naturally interact with others. This seems like common-sense, but it is not always the case. Often people are treated as we would like to be treated. Isn't that what we are told as children? This is nice when it comes to treating people with kindness versus rudeness, but it may do our relationships a lot of good if we are aware and begin to treat others as *they* would like to be treated.

Back to rewarding good behavior, whether it be high fives, hugs, or saying "great job." We reward good behavior because we know it will encourage the same behavior in the future. We must now learn to modify our way of communicating to offer subtle and effective rewards which help to change the dynamic of a relationship. When we become more aware of when others do something we like, rather than focusing on the times they do things which irritate us, we must give ourselves the ability to pause and change our inner dialog and approach situations differently. Keeping in mind that problems are not solved when addressed with anger. A thoughtful and considerate approach will help change our relationships. Evidently, it also releases pressure. It releases pressure inside us, and on the person we are speaking to, and the relationship overall.

I will again use a conversation with my friend Danique as an example: She is one of those friends that I always find myself having conversations which challenge my thinking and change my perspective. It was not until months after this particular conversation I was rereading the book *The 5 Love Languages* by Gary Chapman, that I realized she had not only read the same book as I, but she had successfully implemented its principles into her relationship.

When I first read Chapman's book, it was based on a recommendation of a friend. She had recently begun dating again after going through a divorce and was telling me about the book for "singles" she was reading at the time. That day I went home and did a little research and found that Chapman did not only write about love languages for singles, but also for people in different stages of relationships. I went out and bought the version I thought would best help me. My friend had briefly explained the concepts she had learned during her reading, and it seemed like something that might shed some light on my relationship with my husband. I apparently didn't fully grasp all that I had read during my first read through. I was too busy being caught up in my aha moments of *YES! That's me!* I missed a lot of the advice that could have helped our relationship reading the book initially because my inner dialog while I read focused on the points I related to as an individual, not a couple. I discovered in my second reading that my mind was quieter and in a much better place to learn *how* to implement what I learned, not just be amazed by it.

During my chat with Danique, she explained how she had changed her relationship and her own mental state. She told me a story about her significant other and a habit he had of leaving the kitchen cupboard doors open. I realized that I found her story so motivating because of my prior reading. My conversation with Danique taught me how to utilize Chapman's principles in my own life. It took on a new meaning coming from someone I knew personally, and I was able to understand the effects from someone first hand.

When discussing how habits, which at the beginning of a relationship were "no big deal," Danique and I both agreed that these turn into *big* deals down the road. You know the little things that can drive us crazy? Whether it be underwear on the floor, dishes on the counter, and so on, they are minor in the whole scheme of things. However, they create feelings of resentment, frustration, anger, and annoyance when paired with sick kids, busy jobs, a lack of intimacy, and so much more. After weeks, months, or even years of being bothered by seemingly minor habits, we see them snowball and initiate larger conflicts.

Back to the cupboard doors. Danique recognized that becoming angry every time she entered the kitchen and saw a door left open was not solving the problem. She began to approach it mindfully. She purposefully and softly praised her husband when she saw him shut the cupboard doors. This took emotional control and mindfulness through all the times he didn't close them and explicit and intentional action when he did. Danique used both verbal and physical rewards to reinforce the positive behavior of her husband. When he shut the door she went into the kitchen, and with a soft tone of voice and soft touch, she simply said, "I appreciate it and feel respected when you shut the cupboard doors." With this, she kissed him on the cheek and walked away. I loved that she acknowledged how his actions made her feel, that she communicated clearly and that she did not dwell on it. She quietly walked away and left him to feel loved and appreciated. The next time he was in the kitchen he was far more likely to close the doors having had a positive experience doing so than if she had walked in and scolded him for something that he did not personally prioritize or focus on.

An important part of having the ability to react to others consciously, with less charged emotion, and more constructive conversation, is recognizing our feelings when we assume negative intention where it does not belong. I discussed this briefly in the example of the newly-wed couple doing chores. I will dig deeper into it now.

We often apply negative intention where there was no direct intention at all. When we do, we often can't see the forest for the trees. When negative emotion takes hold, we see the action of the person and perceive it to be deliberately directed at us. While working with horses, I see this all the time. People attribute their horse's response to pressure as a personal attack on them. It is when they move beyond this limited thinking that they open up a balanced and healthy relationship. If people can learn to remove the idea of perceived negative intentions on horses and people alike, they will live happier lives overall. We cannot look to release pressure and reward behavior if we are reacting defensively to the behavior as a result of our thoughts, rather than the reality of the situation.

As much with horses as with humans, we become much more empathetic in our interactions when we try to look at a response from a detached perspective. When we remove ourselves from the situation by changing our perspective, we have the ability to control the thoughts which create hurt and negative feelings. We are open to see the situation for what it truly is, and that is the other individual responding from a place of their own experiences, emotions, and perspective.

When we shift to more conscious communication, we open up our interactions to become more about the other person and less about ourselves. We allow space to respond from a place of genuine empathy. When we respond from a place of genuine empathy, we establish relationships driven by connection, trust, and respect. With horses, this opens the door to a connection that people see in movies and dream about as they enter the pasture. With humans, it opens the door to limitless possibilities with love, friendship, and business.

Allow me to paint a picture for you that exemplifies assuming negative intentions of a stranger and one that should help us become more mindful in similar situations:

We find ourselves rushing to work and are feeling the pressure of the clock and the judgmental glares of coworkers if we stroll in late. We are driving through town on a busy morning, and a gentleman apparently fails to check his left side and cuts us off. Immediately we get a rush of adrenaline and emotion as we project our already negative emotions onto the situation. We automatically begin yelling rude comments at the man, calling him an idiot or worse, and feeling as though he planned to piss us off. We then hold onto the feeling both physically and emotionally long after the incident. The first thing we do when we finally arrive to work is find someone to complain to about how some jerk made us late because he pulled out in front of us and didn't even bother to look. How he didn't acknowledge that he had cut us off, and just did it to make our day even worse. *Note, the use of the word "just" there.*

Our venting does two things for us in this situation: It allows us to feel justified in our reaction to the situation and our feelings toward the man, as well as it makes us feel like we do not have to claim responsibility for being late because it was clearly this other person's fault. If the person we are venting to makes us feel validated by their response, we will feel even more justified and become even more detached from the reality of the situation.

When we are more mindful, and as a result often more positive, we can see the forest past the trees. We see the larger picture: The person likely did not make us upset on purpose. Instead, they made an error with no ill intent and were not conscious that it was even made. When we are mindful, we are also able to take responsibility in situations which result in a much healthier internal dialog. We can see that we were distracted by our thoughts and were driving too quickly for traffic in our rushed state. We also could have made some changes to our morning routine to make our morning more efficient and have us arriving on time to work.

Let's revisit the scenario from the other person's point of view. This will show the value of considering the perspective of others from a wider lens:

The man was in his mid-sixties and lost sight in his left eye due to a work accident one year prior. He spent his recovery time dependent on others. He was uncomfortable with this because he was a man from a generation which believed that men take care of their families and do not need to be taken care of. During his healing, he slipped into a depression that prolonged his recovery and put stress on his marriage. When he was given the okay to drive again, he felt a part of himself return. He thought it would be the answer to regaining control of his life and re-stabilizing his relationship. When he woke on the first day of his new freedom he grabbed the keys to his truck while his wife quietly slept. He approached his vehicle from the driver's side for the first time since his accident. When he turned the key in the ignition and placed his hands on the wheel, he was surprised how something so familiar could feel so foreign. He reached with his right hand, slightly turning his head to the left to grasp his seat belt and fell short. He turned his head with a little more deliberation to see his belt and sighed in exhaustion, not from a lack of sleep, rather a lack of patience for his new limitation. He twisted his whole body to the left, clutched the belt in his hand, pulled it hastily across his lap, and buckled it. Today he was regaining his normal life, starting with the happiness in his home. He pulled out of his driveway and drove twenty minutes to town on quiet roads. He knew navigating through town would be more challenging, but he also knew how much his wife would appreciate the gesture of a fresh bouquet of flowers. This would be his way of saying thank you and a way to brighten up a home that has seen so much darkness in the last year.

After buying the perfect bouquet, one that looked fresh and clean, one that said love, not romance, he maneuvered through the parking lot that was becoming increasingly congested without a problem. Stopped at the exit and out of habit, an old muscle memory response in the midst of a distracting thought, he glanced to his left. He saw no oncoming traffic and pulled out onto the road. Still immersed in thought, he did not recognize his error. His glance was not sufficient for his impaired vision, and he did not see the car he pulled out in front of. He continued to drive, feeling accomplished and in control, straight home to a wife who was sitting on their porch. She managed to push the worry out of her smile as he pulled back into their driveway for the first time since the day she received the call that he had been hurt. She patiently waited for him to get out of his truck and walk to the deck. Despite her frequent need to ask if he needed help, she stood when he reached the steps partly to be there to catch his arm if he tripped and partly to get to him sooner. He presented her the flowers with pride. She kissed him softly and stopped herself from grasping the back of his arm to offer support. That morning also made her realize that this was the start of their journey back to happiness.

You may be thinking that was slightly dramatic for trying to show the importance of not projecting our emotions onto others by fabricating false intentions. Maybe so. However, it was necessary. You see, this situation could have happened to any of us, and hypothetically, to this day, that gentleman does not know he cut us off. If he did, his day would have been shifted to a place of guilt and self-doubt rather than pride and confidence. He did not intend to make our heart jump and our emotions soar, and he did not deserve the slew of insults we hurled in his direction. He did not know. If he did, he would be sorry, not an asshole like we called him.

It is in situations like this that we need to release our own pressure. We create the pressure as a result of circumstances beyond our control that we allow to take hold of us. The stress manifests negative emotions which spill over into other aspects of our lives.

Some may say that it is healthy to get our emotions out and not hold in our feelings. No harm was done by screaming profanities in our car. That is, however, wrong. The harm was not done to the man who cut us off. The harm was done to ourselves. Our negative mindset and our lack of conscious and purposeful thought created a wave of negative emotions that washed over us like salt water. We tasted it for the rest of the day. It immediately changed our vibration; the energy we sent out to the universe. It created a day that we couldn't wait to leave behind. We held onto that feeling until we saw our partner stroll in late that night. Rather than asking them how their day was and why they got home so late, we just got up and glared at them. Our feelings magnified. We fell asleep without speaking to them that night and thought about it as soon as our eyes opened the next morning. We think of how terribly our day started yesterday and how it ended. We continue to hold ourselves in a low, slow-moving vibration. We do not get control of our inner dialog and our ego feeds us stories of hurt and pain and convinces us that we are living an unhappy life.

It is that simple. Had we braked quickly because the truck cut us off, simply spoke a thank you for not being hit, and arrived to work thinking of the job to be done rather than the fear that we felt, we would have felt more compassionate when our partner arrived four hours late. We would have discovered they ran out of gas, and their cell phone had died, and they needed to have something to eat and a hug.

I hope you see the implications of assigning false negative intention on behalf of those around you. In the case of a stranger upsetting you, rewarding good behavior is not necessarily possible. However, if we become cognizant of our own thoughts and the ill intent we place on the actions of others we will have the ability to respond empathetically with everyone and recognize good behavior, which we can reward those closest to us for.

When we do not acknowledge and control our inner dialog, we will find ourselves feeling hurt by others when there was no hurt intended. We shift our mood and miss the opportunity to reward someone when they do something pleasing. When we allow our thoughts to run on autopilot, we will find ourselves regularly frustrated, annoyed, and often judgmental. Once again, when we are more mindful of our thoughts and emotional reactions we tend to be more empathetic, understanding, and positive.

Thoughts lead to emotion. When we allow our automatic thoughts to remain unchecked, we have ideas pop into our head as we perceive the world around us and lead us to feel whatever emotion those thoughts correlate with. Our minds are continually searching for meaning. It is the meaning of an event that our thoughts decipher, which results in how we feel. If someone cuts us off, we think we are being put in danger. We feel fear and sometimes anger. If we see a significant other look at someone else who we think they may find attractive, we may perceive this as a threat that they might leave us. We begin to feel inadequate, mistreated, jealous, or resentful. Our automatic thoughts *"can be words, an image, a memory, a physical sensation, an imagined sound, or based on our intuition or a sense of just knowing."*[10]

We tend to believe our thoughts without question of their credibility. Every thought we think is not always true, authentic, or valuable. Our thoughts tend to repeat, and we all know that repetition creates a habit; something we have to change consciously. Our thoughts are easy to believe because our experiences and our perceptions form them. They are what guides us throughout our days.

So how do we decipher if a thought is trustworthy? We ask if our thought is our opinion or if it is a fact. You will know the difference because facts are driven by rational thought and are based on evidence. Opinions are based on a number of influencing factors that are often assumed rather than proven. They are induced and strengthened by emotion. Mindfulness requires an open and flexible mind. This allows breakthroughs, improvement, and growth. With more conscious thought we will begin to see how our moods often shadow our views and we will start to interact and respond from a different perspective.

I think it is important to recognize that there are times when we feel like we can't get away from the negative feelings which build up. Being mindful does not eliminate difficult times in our lives nor will it eradicate all conflict, feelings of sadness, or hurt. It will not sugar coat our lives.

So, how can we release our negative emotions without them coming out in non-constructive ways like overreacting, overwhelming feelings of resentment, or actions which result in a cycle of negativity? Again, self-awareness is key.

You can do a number of things to release the tension, but

it will depend on what works best for you. For instance, some people love running, they feel free and at peace when they run. Not me though! I never found the euphoric state others speak of when they go for a run. I have never enjoyed it and likely never will. So it would be wise for me to release my tension through another activity; one which allows me to release the tension and give me the energy needed to shift my mood and perspective by shifting me to a place closer to joy. Some activities I would suggest are: physical activity (with so many options in itself, such as swimming, dancing, walking, lifting weights, horseback riding, gardening, sight-seeing, yoga, anything to get you off your ass and on your feet), writing/journaling, talking to a friend (make sure they are a supporter, not an enabler), barn chores, fishing, or meditating. You get the point.

We need to find something we truly enjoy and can get lost doing. Then we need to set aside time to do it. Taking time for ourselves is necessary. We cannot run on empty. When we do, we become most entangled in unnecessary conflict, drama, and negativity.

Look for the Try

This book was in its final draft when I realized that I had something to add to this chapter. This idea came to me during a conversation I had with my husband. The discussion was one that comes up every so often when things fall out of balance; when life begins to divide us, and we allow the daily grind to override the importance of a happy relationship. I was feeling very sensitive and reactive around my husband, and he was feeling frustrated and mistreated by my responses to him. I was, clearly, not in the most conscious state of communication at this time, and I admit this freely.

I can look to blame many things: I was stressed with the upcoming completion of my book, I was consumed by my efforts to be all the things required of me, and I was being spread too thin as a result. I was feeling disconnected from him and a little lonely in our relationship and a few others. Rather than blame all these things, I needed to recognize that I had lost touch with mindfulness, not only within my communication with my husband but also with myself. I allowed my thoughts to control my emotions and my feelings were certainly running away with me.

Let me explain. When I allowed myself to disconnect from communicating from a conscious and mindful place, I only saw the big picture, and I was missing all the great things along the way. I was missing all the little places to release my pressure, for both myself and my husband, and I successfully frustrated and overwhelmed the both of us by doing so.

When we are teaching our students about working through challenges with their horse not wanting to complete an obstacle, we touch on this very problem. I can see when someone is only seeing the end goal and graying their communication as a result of becoming frustrated by unmet expectations and unnecessary emotional responses.

I use the example of having a person ask their horse to cross the water box on a regular basis. A water box is usually a challenging obstacle that is typically made from a 4x8 foot sheet of plywood with four-inch sides to hold a few inches of water. This obstacle sounds easy but tends to be a challenge for a fair amount of horses and is the cause of much frustration for just as many riders. As we explain how to best get through the water box with the highest rate of success and the least amount of argument, we encourage our riders to forget about the end goal of walking through the box. Instead, they should think of asking the horse to walk up to the box straight, offering a yes when asked to take a step forward. We have them focus on one step at a time. What this allows them to do is to see and feel their horse's *try*, which is exactly when we tell them to release their pressure and reward their horse.

When a person is present enough to see and feel each try from their horse they communicate with appropriate pressure and release, they usually get to the other side of the water box before they thought they could and if not, then most certainly with less or no fight. By looking to reward our horses on their try, we work them in a much more positive mindset and are looking for the good instead of focusing on the bad, the refusals. When we shift our focus this way, our horses have an opportunity to work through our pressure with the thinking side of their brain and are more likely to respond than to react.

My realization after hitting a communication block within my marriage was that I had written a whole book that discussed applying methods we use on horses to our relationships, and I had almost considered it complete without recognizing one of the most important ones. I allowed my end goal and emotionally charged expectations to take away all my feel and create a dramatic situation that could have been completely prevented.

This shows something pretty important though. When we are teaching, I routinely see the damage that is done to the communication when the person does not recognize the horse's tries. However, I could not see how damaging it was to my own relationship. I hadn't even thought to implement this into my own communication with people. I believe that is because I have come to feel it so naturally with horses. As it turns out, I was no better than a frustrated horse owner kicking the ground by my horse and swearing with gritted teeth at the entrance of the water box, missing every effort and try made by my partner.

I was so caught up in my own world that I could not see all my husband's small tries to offer me exactly what I wanted, and had been asserting were absolutely necessary, for my happiness or satisfaction. I failed to notice when he tried to be soft with me, something I have told him is important so many times. I missed when he tried to show me affection that had no strings attached, just good ole bits of communication that sang "I love you" through nicknames, attempts at lighthearted jokes, hugs, handholds, and so much more. I was so busy telling him that he was not listening that I missed all the times he was. *Damn.*

With this new-found revelation, I also discovered that I was feeling emotional and overwhelmed with him due to the *exact* same problem. Both of us were applying so much pressure on the other that all the efforts and tries on each other's part were being missed and resulting in both of us feeling completely out of touch in our marriage. I am not happy that we went through this stage of unconscious communication, but I'm not entirely unhappy about it either. I am grateful that it taught me a lesson I needed to learn. I am also glad that I was able to show that we are always growing, we are never perfect, and our relationships, no matter how enlightened we are becoming, will still have highs and lows.

I could have left this part out. I could have come to this conclusion and discussed it in private with my man and pretended it never happened. After all, how do I admit that I had a small hole in my relationship because of poor communication when I had just written a book on it? Believe me, I thought about it. Then I remembered that hiding as a result of shame would never enable me to create the connection I desire in my life with others.

Brené Brown's term "Going Back" in her book, *I thought It Was Just Me (but it isn't): Making the Journey from "What Will People Think?" To "I Am Enough"* came back to me here.[11] Brown's book taught me that "*The ability to learn from our mistakes rather than seeing them as failed attempts at perfection is the essence of 'going back.'*"[12] I believe going back is what allows me to continue to have faith in my abilities even when I make mistakes. Mistakes are cause for reflection and growth. There are many times I would love to pretend all of my mistakes are a result of others' actions allowing me to pass off responsibility and lay blame. Man, it would be awesome to do that and save myself the vulnerable conversations and all the feelings that go with learning from my mistakes, but I would live a much less empathetic, connected, and aligned life with who I am and want to become. I want to be my most authentic self, and that will never happen while hiding behind my shame and fear.

I will end this chapter with another powerful insight from Brené Brown, "*We cannot share ourselves with others when we see ourselves as flawed and unworthy of connection. It's impossible to be 'real' when we are ashamed of who we are or what we believe.*"[13]

When we recognize what builds negative pressure within ourselves we also gain insight into the burden we place on others. We have the power over our thoughts and can prevent unnecessary stress, anxiety, and grief in every situation we encounter. When we meet life with a compassionate heart rather than a defensive one, we are better able to see the good that surrounds us, especially the good other people bring into our lives. It is only then that we can create a true connection within our relationships.

Exercise:

In your journal write down three things that your significant other, close friend, or family does which cause you to feel frustrated, hurt, or unappreciated.

Now, write down what you will say to them when you catch them doing something that makes you happy. Some examples are:

- "I appreciate it when you do that. Thank you."

- "I love it when you see how hard I worked today and help keep things clean/tidy."

- "This is why I married you. You are so thoughtful."

- "I know you are in a rush, and I want to say thank you for taking the time for _____. It makes me feel appreciated."

- "Thank you for the effort you put into helping me. You are a great man/woman/partner/sister/etc."

I want you to use clear and concise language. I want them to know exactly what they did that you liked and how it made you feel. Feel free to plan how or where you will touch them. Of course, depending on the nature of your relationship, things may get awkward if you slid your hand into your coworkers back pocket! The important thing to know is that deliberate talk and touch can be the best reward someone can receive for doing something they didn't even know or feel was important when they were doing it.

The next time you see them do the very thing you wrote down that frustrates you or brings up negative emotion; I want you to observe them and then ask yourself these questions:

- What caused them to do what they were doing? Were they rushed? Feeling emotionally charged themselves? Were they distracted? Were they tired? Were they doing it out of habit? Were they on autopilot?

- Why do their actions frustrate me? Does it create more work for me? Does it convey to me that I am not valued? Does it communicate to me that they have not retained anything from a conversation or argument we had?

- Is my negative emotional reaction their intent? Think as rationally as you can here. If you do believe so, you will have to uncover why that is and it likely says more about your relationship and the other person than it does about you as an individual. It also leads to our next topic—stay tuned!

Write down your answers later that evening and be conscious of your rational thought. Answer as if you are an onlooker who is not emotionally attached to the situation.

Now, BREATHE. Accept the moment for what it is. Think of one thing they do that you love and say thank you to yourself for it. Maybe tomorrow is the day they put their clothes in the hamper and not beside it. When they do, you are going to casually and effectively acknowledge their action and move on.

A great reminder for you to breathe through those moments is to write the word BREATHE on your hand or arm where you can see it for a few days. It will help create a pause in your thoughts and allow you to shift your energy from frustrated to patient.

Take a moment to write down a few options for releasing negative emotions and tension from your body and try to schedule at least one of these activities into your week.

CHAPTER THREE

Respect is Not Transferable

"You teach people how to treat you by what you allow, what you stop, and what you reinforce."

Tony Gaskins

The number one lesson in the horse world is that you teach others how to treat you. Trainers see it all the time. A horse can be soft and responsive with the trainer and in a few minutes, days, weeks, or months after the horse returns to their owner the trainer may receive a call or message stating that the horse is not the same anymore. The horse may have become pushy again or difficult to handle in one way or another, but the main thing is they aren't *the same*. The horse is not maintaining the same desired behaviors for the owner as they had for the trainer. Often this is solely blamed on a lack of respect for the owner on the horse's part; however, that is not entirely true. Remember, trust and respect go hand in hand. The trainer likely gained the respect of the horse because the horse could trust that they were a consistent leader. Often, gray communication creates confusion and frustration for a horse that later gets blamed for lack of respect. The horse has learned how to behave with its owner based on their body language and their response to situations while handling them or riding them.

It is crucial for me to note here: When we function in relationships where we are more concerned with gaining respect than trust, the relationship is bound to encounter impasses. The same applies to people. Each person you interact with learns first how they can treat you by your body language, your first impression, and second by your interactions. If you want to learn more about our body language and the science behind it, among many other aspects of human nature and the science behind it, I suggest you check out Vanessa Van Edwards. Her book is called *Captivate: The Science of Succeeding with People.*[14] As a horse person who is invested in learning how my body language speaks to a horse, it was intriguing to read how it applies to people. Feel free to laugh at me for having not given much thought to body language between humans until I had truly discovered its importance with horses.

As social beings, we develop a level of trust and respect through seeing, hearing, and interacting with others. When we perceive them and our interactions with them to be fair and consistent, we feel safe and hold them in high regard. When we do not feel someone treats others or ourselves fairly and consistently, we lack respect for them because we think they are dishonest, unpredictable, and unreliable.

When a horse shows signs of disrespect or a lack of trust, it is because they do not feel they can rely on the human to keep them safe. They will feel like they have to fend for themselves and take matters into their own "hands." This is similar to how children respond to adults. It all comes down to communication. We must be clear and consistent for others to trust and respect us. With both horses and humans, if our communication skills are lacking, they won't understand or trust us and will feel the need to run the show.

Teaching high school taught me this valuable lesson as well. I learned that just because I saw a student act respectfully in another classroom or with another adult that did not mean that was how they would act in my room or with me in the hallway. It is assumptions such as this which set teachers off on a wrong foot with many students. As we know, assuming anything "makes an ass out of you and me."

We need to teach others that we can be trusted and the respect will follow. We need to create a connection. The same goes for adult relationships. There is another contributing factor that influences how others treat us in our relationships, whether they speak to us mindfully and with respect for our feelings, and that is our response to them when they do not do so.

I have seen relationships built on trust and respect change over time due to a lack of clear communication of boundaries. The "offender" may not understand how they are making us feel because we have never communicated it or we were unclear in our communication when we tried. They may behave toward us in a joking manner that they perceive as funny or playful. In spite of this, we may find that hurtful or offensive. Often, when we speak up for ourselves, we shed light on others' behavior that they did not see as hurtful and ideally it shifts them into more mindful interactions. Sometimes, unfortunately, it results in them feeling defensive of their actions because they are not able to accept responsibility at that time for one personal reason or another. We feel better about our relationship almost immediately when the person is able to see things from our perspective and this helps build the trust and respect we seek despite disagreements or misunderstandings. No matter the relation, close or simply an acquaintance, we have to be clear about how we want to be treated in order for the relationship to be founded on mutual trust and respect. It is here I encourage you to give yourself permission to change how you want to be treated in a relationship.

Often, when we fail to set clear boundaries for ourselves, we end up in situations that make us feel used, mistreated or threatened. When situations like this occur, we then go through a range of emotions resulting from the experience.

While I was writing this chapter I was reminded of a situation that happened to me a few years ago that made me acutely aware of how the lack of boundaries not only affects the relationship between those who are personally involved, but also others who surround them.

I had made an obligation to attend an important event. The event was something that held great importance to me and required me to be there in a professional manner. My being there not only influenced myself and my business but others as well. Unfortunately, the man who was hosting it had just recently had a falling out with a friend of mine. My friend was very hurt by the way the host had treated him throughout the days leading up to the event and felt the loyalty of others to him, shown by a lack of support to the other guy's event, would teach him a lesson.

My friend requested that I change my plans. I didn't think this was a smart business move for myself and this made me appear to be more involved in the situation than I truly was. I did not mind supporting my friend as he worked his way through the drama that they had created, but I was not willing to become an active participant in it. When I told him as clearly and kindly as I could that I would still be attending the event he was upset because he was searching for support and searching for justice. He let me know in words and a tone that were very emotionally charged that

I should not be supporting this person. My friend thought that my withdrawal from this event would show my loyalty to him and teaching the offending person that they were wrong in how they treated my friend. They wanted me to teach the other person a lesson.

Let me say here; I think loyalty is a value to hold to high esteem, however being loyal to a friend at the detriment to myself is not doing either of us any good. I listened to him as he told me how much it hurt that I was choosing to do this and I stayed true to my reason why.

A few weeks later when we sat over coffee, I explained to him what I thought as he told me weeks ago how hurt he was by my actions. I did not tell him these things when we talked before the event because he was not in a place to receive what I wanted to say without becoming defensive. He needed time to let the situation dissipate, and the wound to be less fresh. I told him in our conversation that I needed him to know that I am not responsible to teach others how to treat him. That is his responsibility. It simply was not my lesson to teach.

For months leading up to the final confrontation between my friend and the event host, I had been offering advice and insights about how he was being treated. I had said numerous times that boundaries were clearly not set between them and if they were, they certainly were not being reinforced. I could see the situation escalating from an outside perspective for weeks and nothing I said then fixed it, so if my advice did not help the situation while it was unraveling, whether I attended this event or not, it was not going to change how these two individuals perceived or treated each other.

In regards to the boundaries we set with people, much as the same as everything that comes with personal growth, we may find ourselves in a state where something that once felt acceptable, or even good for us, no longer serves that purpose. This is where we offer long-term relationships a chance of existing. Our boundaries can change just as we can change. In reality, our boundaries must change as we change to ensure that we are surrounding ourselves with people who help us move forward, not those who hold us back.

People do not remain in relationships, romantic or not, for long periods of time without coping with change. They maintain these relationships by communicating *through* change. The trust and respect they have established facilitate healthy shifts in how they interact. We cannot expect ourselves or others to stay the same our whole lives. We must love them deeper, beyond what or who they presently are and use that love to promote meaningful communication through change.

I will use another personal experience as an example here: I began dating my husband at the end of my first year of being a classroom teacher. I was young and energized and still convinced that I could change the lives of *all* of my students.

Seven years into our relationship, and only about a month into our marriage, I went to my first workshop for women that focused on our power to change our lives through the understanding of the law of attraction and meditation. I felt something inside me shift. I became obsessed with understanding what was holding me back from my greatest desires. I began reading, taking courses, and connecting with like-minded people. I learned a lot about myself and what my dreams were. I changed.

I decided to leave a full-time teaching position to follow a new calling. Rather than resist the change, my husband supported me through it. The best part of my shift was a shift in us. My new confidence brought us to a new point in our relationship where communication became easier between us and the business we work together began to take off.

I am not the same woman he began dating. I know he loves me more today than ever. Not all partners accept change from their spouse like mine did and I am forever grateful. Thinking about the what if's around this topic can be a bit scary, but it is important to do so. Not only does this allow us to be consciously grateful for what is, but it tunes us into how we would feel if it was not.

What if my husband did not support the changes I made? I love him, and I cannot picture my life without him, but I also have finally had the courage to love myself and to change my life to allow myself to live more aligned with who I am. It hurts even to write it, but I would have to remain true to myself to continue on a path of seeking joy. I simply could not place his temporary happiness over my lifetime of happiness. I would have to walk my new path without him, or at least in a different way. Writing this is an excellent reminder to me of how truly remarkable he is, and it makes my heart happy knowing that my "I dos" didn't result in me feeling like there are "I don'ts" when it comes to my hopes, dreams, and desires.

Don't panic; I am not saying here that I would have chosen to leave my husband if he told me that we could not afford for me to leave my teaching career. That being said, I would expect him to still understand and look for ways to support me in my struggle. If leaving had not been an option for us at that time, I would not want him to shut down the possibility of it ever happening, just for the time being. If his response was, "We can't have that happen right now, but let's set a plan in place to help get us to a better spot financially in a few years and then we can be comfortable with the decision. In the meantime, what can we do to make you happier on a daily basis?" Then I would know he was working with me, not against me.

The acknowledgment of struggle and the desire to help fix it, even if helping means allowing the other space and time of their own to do the fixing, is so important in a healthy, supportive, and balanced relationship. If this had not been my husband's response, I would have to take time to communicate as clearly as possible my need for his support and then continue to assess things from there.

I don't want anyone to think from this example that I would take the decision to end a marriage lightly or that I would run off because my husband did not agree with what I wanted to do, but the fact that unhealthy or unsupportive relationships hold people in unhappy, misaligned lives is very much a reality. It takes a lot of conscious internal communication to truly establish the limits of any relationship. Above all, your mental, emotional, and physical health should be a top priority for you and your partner. If this is not the case, then some very clear communication is required.

Other examples of how a shift in a relationship can create a distinct need for deliberate conversation could be a couple who goes from casually dating to a more exclusive relationship, it could be going from living separately to then sharing a home, or it could be from being a married couple with children to a divorced couple who co-parent. All of these relationships have gone through a transition, and throughout that transition boundaries inevitably change. It is common for people to change their expectations of a person within a relationship, yet they never talk to that person about the change in those expectations because they feel like the other person should *just* know. This sort of thinking is asking for conflict and hurt feelings.

We also cannot assume that others have the same values within the confines of specific types of relationships as we do. To make this clear, we can look at how unspoken changes in expectations can cause conflict for a couple who have newly moved in together. This is a big one. This will show a couple if they are as compatible as they think. When a couple chooses to spend time together on a semi-regular basis, they learn a lot of the things they love or admire about each other. When couples move in together their worlds collide. It is here where we begin to find areas that may be deemed incompatible. Rather than taking the time to discuss expectations we often assume that the other knows, or the most damaging, that they *should* know.

When we assume someone should know something, like how to treat us, it causes negative emotions such as resentment and frustration where they do not belong. Most of us only communicate what we expect from a relationship after we have been disappointed and feel let down. It is common for people to express they are unhappy in their marriage or a relationship with a friend because the relationship isn't what they thought or expected it to be. More often than not, *expectations are thrown like knives during an argument.* As discussed previously, we know that words spoken in anger do not solve problems, so it is no wonder that when expectations are only spoken in frustration that they will likely not get met in the future.

If we want to set our relationships up for success we must communicate our expectations prior to the situations where we feel they should be met. The only problem is we often don't know we have even placed certain expectations on people until we have feelings of frustration or disappointment. That tends to be when we use defensive excuses such as, "I shouldn't have to tell you, you should already know!"

How are others supposed to know our expectations when we don't even know them ourselves? Sadly, we let it build inside of us like the perfect storm and then finally allow it all to surface in a violent, angry, or emotionally charged manner resulting in nothing constructive or helpful.

It has been proven that people learn best when they have to teach their knowledge to others.[15] I believe this is why some of us learn so well and invest in our knowledge for our animals; we are learning with the intention to teach the animal. If we could apply this to our interactions with the people in our lives, we would prioritize learning how to communicate. We would be learning in order to teach others how to communicate with us effectively. When you learn to implement the concepts in this book into your own life and teach others how to treat you, you will feel empowered through educating and strengthening your relationships.

So, let's say you have determined your expectations in your mind and you want to communicate them with your partner or friend. How do you go about it without them assigning negative intention to your actions? The answer is clear communication. Remember, when teaching horsemanship we say, *"Be gentle in what you do, yet firm in how you do it."* This brings us back to the chapter on softness.

In case you missed the quote at the beginning of Chapter One, I will repeat it here, written by Victoria Erickson, *"Just because you are soft doesn't mean that you are not a force."* This speaks to my soul, and I hope you derive meaning from it too. But the question is, how do we accomplish this? This is done by setting boundaries and holding people accountable from a place of compassion, understanding, and confidence. If we do not set clear boundaries, then people do not know what is expected of them. If we do not hold people accountable, then no one will take our boundaries seriously and will not respect them as such.

It is vital that we do not attribute the use of the word boundaries with something negative. It is not at all. The terms boundaries and barriers often get used interchangeably. It is important that we do not confuse these two. Boundaries allow for clear communication whereas barriers restrict communication.

Boundaries allow us to be on the same page with everyone around us. They eliminate unspoken expectations which we know can be lethal to our relationships. Your boundaries may not be favorable to everyone. After all, I didn't say that they wouldn't be perceived as negative by others, rather they shouldn't be regarded as negative by yourself. That being said, boundaries that are created and communicated from a place of vulnerability and truth should all be respected in healthy relationships. Maybe not 100% liked, but certainly respected. People will trust and respect us more if we communicate clear boundaries and stick to them.

We cannot build relationships based on trust and respect if we set barriers to hide behind, which we often do because we are afraid of the vulnerability we will feel when communicating those expectations. Barriers differ from boundaries because they cause negative emotions such as confusion, resentment, and pain.

We can tell if we are creating barriers rather than boundaries because we will avoid communication for fear of confrontation. When we put barriers in place, we will be compelled to move further away from the conflict. When we set boundaries, on the other hand, we are required to move toward the issues that make us uncomfortable because that is where a boundary or line has to be drawn. When we are sure, and in tune with the boundaries we have set, we will feel empowered and will not be afraid to confront others about sensitive issues. We will confidently assert ourselves when needed.

Setting boundaries comes from a place of self-love and self-awareness. They are also communicated from a place of love. We must dig deep and be honest with our feelings to create boundaries true to who we are, and to help establish as well as maintain healthy and happy relationships.

When I work with people and their horses, it is evident when barriers are set rather than boundaries. People who set barriers with their horses demand respect and allow their emotional response to control their actions with their horse. They move away from interacting with their horse from a place of love and compassion to a place of control and ego. When people handle horses from a place of "I'll teach you!" they assert unnecessary or unwarranted pressure on the horse which confuses communication and causes the horse to react in fear rather than trust and respect. The same happens with people.

We cannot teach others how to treat us when we interact from a place of control and ego. This does not allow us to respond compassionately. This usually leads to us placing blame rather than communicating from a place of taking perspective and opening up a constructive conversation.

Not all boundaries are created equally. It is important for us to know when we have set what I will refer to as flexible or hard boundaries.

Flexible versus Hard Boundaries

Flexible boundaries are important to establish because they allow the people around us to make mistakes. They enable us to approach these mistakes with empathy and understanding, yet still will enable us to communicate clearly when a boundary of ours has been crossed. It is important to note that having flexible boundaries does not mean you change or modify your boundaries as a result of others' actions. However, these boundaries are worth reassessing at times to ensure that they are still in tune with the stages of growth in your life.

Flexible boundaries open up conversations that give way to second chances and teach others how to love you. When we communicate through the times our flexible boundaries have been broken, the ramifications of the conversation are generally not life-altering. An example of a flexible boundary being crossed is this:

You find out you just got a job you applied for. You hadn't told anyone you applied because you were worried you would jinx it by telling people, and you didn't want to have to explain it to anyone if you didn't get the job. So you kept it to yourself, despite your excitement. When you find out you have been selected, you call up your best friend, Jill. She is your go-to girl, and you need to tell someone before you burst.

When you tell Jill, she seems a bit off. Her voice is short, and she has a tone of annoyance even though she is saying all the right things. You chalk her tone up to something her husband must have done or said to annoy or upset her. You continue telling her about what the new job will mean for you, besides moving to another country, and her tone seems to grow more impatient. You catch the hint that she isn't in the mood to talk and remind her not to tell anyone because you haven't told your mom yet. She assures you that your secret is safe with her and she hangs up before you are even done saying goodbye.

Over the next few days, you hustle to get your ducks in a row. You spend your time ironing out every detail before you call your mom. She is a planner and you know she will ask every question possible about this choice. You want to be able to supply an answer to every question. You haven't had time to talk to Jill since you told her about your new job earlier in the week. You have a feeling you should call her but, unfortunately, in the rush and excitement, you forget.

Finally, five days after you accepted your new job, you call your mom feeling prepared for whatever she throws your way. When she answers, she is abrupt and you are reminded of your conversation with Jill and how she spoke to you. You carry on the obligatory, "How is so and so?" and questions about regular life then you bite the bullet and reluctantly say, "Mom, I have something to tell you." To which you are met with a, "You don't have to tell me, I already heard." *But how?!* You only told one person. Your mind races on how to put out this fire and your blood pressure rises as you realize how she must have found out.

You try to keep your voice soft and explain to her as clearly as possible why you waited almost a week before telling her you were moving. You reassure her that you wanted to get all the details worked out to avoid causing her extra worry, and you apologize for her finding out before you got to tell her yourself. As she says goodbye after a shorter than anticipated conversation, you hear her voice crack as she says, "I love you." Your heart breaks a little and your mind spins in rage that your best friend could do this to you.

Instead of calling Jill immediately, you decide to take a walk and calm down. Calling her in this state will not do any good. You know her well, and you know she will only become defensive and shut down any communication if you speak to her angrily. You clear your head on your walk and begin to feel your energy shift back into the positive. You decide to call her when you are thinking rationally and with an open heart that is willing to listen.

When you call Jill, she answers almost immediately, sounding a bit better than the last time you spoke, though still far from enthusiastic to hear your voice. You cut right to the chase and simply say, "I just got off the phone with my mom. She hung up crying because she found out I was moving before I was able to tell her myself. Jill, you are the only one I told. I told you not to tell anyone." You leave it at that and wait for her response, praying she will speak openly rather than defensively and you know there is a 50/50 chance.

With her first word, you know this conversation is going to go in the right direction. She says, almost in a whisper, "Oh no, I'm so sorry." You sink into your chair and let out a sigh. You spend the next hour talking and discover why Jill was so short with you the day you last spoke. She knew with the new job that she would be facing changes too. Feeling very out of control in the situation, Jill became resentful rather than excited. She knows she should be encouraging and supportive despite herself.

Nevertheless, her sadness at the thought of "losing" her best friend upon hearing your news overpowered her ability to say what you needed to hear. The reassurance of, "We will still be friends, you aren't losing me," only helps so much. You both know the changes in your address will change daily routines, conversations, and times together.

Having had the much-needed conversation with Jill, you feel

good about the fact that she understands where she overstepped the boundaries of your friendship and that it was done without any ill intent.

If this was one of *many* times you found yourself in conflict or unnecessary drama due to Jill's lack of loyalty to you, the conversation might have turned out very differently. You may have even decided that this was the final straw and this move was the best way to step away from a friendship with someone who clearly does not respect your boundaries and perhaps does not value honesty or loyalty as you do. This is a sign the friendship is not serving you in a positive way.

As you can see from the example above, flexible boundaries allow space for mistakes, and forgiveness, and conversation. You may only have a conversation with a friend about one of your boundaries after it has been crossed the first time. This is okay, although it is crucial you have the conversation about it.

So often someone hurts us in some way through their actions, and we feel slighted by them, but despite this, we wait until the situation occurs multiple times before we address it. Have you ever heard someone say or maybe you have said it, "You *ALWAYS* do this?! Why can't you *just* . . . " If this line is said, or something close to it, and it is the first time you have addressed it, you are part of the problem. How you want to be treated within this, or any, relationship is based on assumptions, not communicated expectations, needs, or desires. If on the other hand, you use the above line having already spoken about this particular action in the past, you need to assess how clearly you are stating your boundary.

If the boundary is clear, you need to assess why the respect is not being upheld. If the boundary is not being upheld then one of you may need to change or move on. You may not need to cut them out of your life entirely; rather you may need to change the dynamics and parameters of your relationship to establish one that does not cause hurt feelings and resentment. In this case, maybe a best friend who you once shared all your secrets with becomes a friend who you enjoy seeing a couple of times a month to share some laughs and hugs; just not secrets and vulnerable information which you have experienced that they do not treat respectfully. You do not have to write off everyone who does not respect the boundaries of your relationship. Sometimes you have to assess the nature of the relationship and change it to have the relationship bring you joy rather than stress.

When we have established and communicated our hard boundaries in a relationship, business and pleasure alike, the chances we offer others to rectify their mistakes should be done so with our feelings and vulnerabilities as our priority, not theirs. At times, we have to be self-focused, often referred to as selfish. Call it what you will, it is vital to our mental health.

Hard boundaries are established by determining our highest values. If we value faithfulness and honesty in a romantic relationship, then this must be communicated clearly at the beginning of the relationship through an open conversation. Within our discussion, we should explain why we feel this way and have set this boundary. As clearly as possible, let them know that it is a deal breaker for this type of relationship if the boundary is crossed.

When we explain our "why" to people it allows them to connect to our needs from a place of empathy and understanding. This also opens up the door for them to communicate their boundaries as well in a safe and genuine conversation.

After we have established trust through our vulnerable and honest conversation, it is then up to us to protect ourselves from people who break that trust through deliberate actions. When this happens, we will not feel less emotion due to communicating our boundaries based on our highest values. In fact, it may hurt more. In these situations, it is so important to love ourselves enough not to bend and break for others.

Often, when hard boundaries are crossed it results in

life-changing decisions. For example, a wife cheats and breaks the trust of her husband, resulting in the husband choosing to end the marriage; a boss makes a sexual advance at their employee while she is working late and she no longer feels safe and decides to transfer to a new branch. Whatever the situation, the trust is broken beyond repair and challenging decisions have to be made as a result.

Remember, a hard boundary for you may be a flexible boundary for someone else. Clear, honest, and empathetic conversation is crucial to come to a mutual understanding in all relationships. Having a conversation about boundaries will offer room for further discussions as the relationship dynamics change, resulting in changes in our boundaries.

We are absolutely allowed to change. Keep this in mind. Experience is our teacher. Take time to process your thoughts and feelings and to communicate them as needed to those who they affect directly. Be sure to explain your "why" to those you have set specific expectations on. Be aware of and communicate your flexible boundaries. Clear conversations lead to growth within relationships and your hard boundaries, which keep you true to yourself, stop you from playing small due to unhealthy relationships.

Exercise:

In order to communicate our boundaries clearly to others, we need to take some time to think about what our values are and what we expect as a result of them.

1. First, we must define our personal values and our fundamental beliefs. These will help us establish what we believe is right and wrong. We may decide we value honesty more than spontaneity, or rationality over open-mindedness.

What is a value?[16]

A value must be freely chosen. Values are a personal choice.

A value shows up in every aspect of our life. We invest time, money, and energy into the things we value.

A value always has alternatives. Choice does not exist without other options to choose from. We do not value things we have no choice over such as needs for survival; food or water.

A value manifests after thoughtful consideration of choices. Impulsive or mindless choices do not lead to true values.

A value has a positive quality. Values result from positive choices we have made.

A value can be expressed publicly. We take pride in our choice.

In your journal, write down your top five values from the example list. Defining your values is empowering and may help you make sense of your actions in the past and present a little better. When you get in touch with the things that matter most to you, you will have the foundation for your boundaries.

Examples of Personal Values

Acceptance	Empathy	Loyalty
Accomplishment	Faith	Optimism
Accountability	Forgiveness	Patience

Ambition	Generosity	Reason
Aspiration	Genuine	Reliability
Caring	Hard Working	Self-Control
Clear Thinking	Honesty	Sensitivity
Commitment	Humility	Supportive
Compassion	Initiative	Thoughtfulness
Competitiveness	Joy	Tolerance
Consistency	Law-Abiding	Tranquility
Courage	Love	Trustworthiness
Dedication	Moderation	Understanding
Dependability	Morals	Wisdom

2. Next, we will determine your limits and thresholds now that we hopefully have a clear picture of what you value. It may be helpful to think of the answers to these questions:

What triggers your stress?

What can or can't you handle emotionally?

What is your limit for tolerating something or someone?

Knowing and defining our limits gives us an idea of what our boundaries will look like. Before we try to communicate what we expect of others, we have to know what our limits are. You may need to take time to think about this or write it down. You may even wish to discuss it with someone you trust and feel comfortable opening up to. As a general rule, a good way to establish your limits is to take note of when you feel angry or mistreated. It is important to be able to recognize what we can handle or tolerate from others and what we simply cannot.

3. Know your power. Our boundaries are for our protection. It is not to make others around you conform to your wants, or your ability to control others. We set boundaries to be treated in ways that maintain healthy relationships; business, romantic, and otherwise. We cannot force someone to trust and respect us. However, clearly and consistently communicating our boundaries will gain trust and respect more consistently than having hidden expectations and inconsistent reactions to actions done by others. We fall into the habit of reacting inconsistently when we allow our thoughts to control our emotions, perceive all our thoughts as true, and never take the time to establish what it is we need/want from the people in our lives.

For example, let's say your significant other always drives you crazy when they walk through the house with dirty boots on. It seems menial, but it happens often enough that you mumble under your breath every time you see it has happened and as you clean it you convince yourself they do it on purpose, to piss you off.

If you were to deal with this inconsistently, you may clean it resentfully but silently one day, then the next day you may totally let loose on them about it and scream at them about how inconsiderate they are as you hastily mop the floor in front of them. Neither of these responses is going to solve the problem, and you will walk away from the situation feeling an array of negative emotions. If you set it as a boundary and decided to address it in a constructive way, it will prevent you from feeling intense negative emotions over something quite small.

Here is the same scenario but with different outcome: You see the boot tracks over your newly cleaned floor for the first time, you sigh because it is annoying, but you do not allow the annoyance to build into resentment. You take it for what it is, a situation you need to talk about, and then move on. Maybe you decide to clean the mess, in which case you do so knowing this is your choice, but not one you will be making in the future, and you will complete the task knowing you will talk to them about it when you both have time to listen that day. When you talk, you do not make them feel stupid or speak to them in a demeaning way. You simply state your case, and it may go something like this, "Oh, before I forget, do you mind slipping your boots off when you forget something and run into the house? If not, the mop is in the closet next to the door. You can quickly wipe up your footprints as you make your way back out. We are teaching our daughter to clean up after herself, and it doesn't set a very good example when we get home to a mess she knows I did not make. Plus, it makes me feel pretty crappy. Thanks for your help."

If you are thinking, *Yeah right! They would NEVER listen to that!* Then that is a pretty good indication that either you have not set boundaries in the past, have responded inconsistently when you have, or they don't show you much respect when you do set healthy boundaries. Either way, it will need to be worked through in order to change your relationship dynamics.

A little side note here: Do not have this conversation over and over again. Do not clean it a second time if you did the first, have them clean it by nicely asking them to. If they don't, or it turns into an issue on their end, then it is showing you have something that needs to be worked on. Approach it mindfully when you do.

On to the next part of the exercise. In your journal:

1. Write the name of a person you have a close relationship with. Write three things you value most about this particular relationship.

2. Pick one of those values and attribute a boundary to it.
   For example, I value honesty in a relationship with my significant other. This value forms the boundary of not being lied to.

3. Write how you can clearly communicate this boundary with the person you desire.
   For example, I will clearly communicate with my partner that honesty is important to me and that even when honesty is hard, and even hurtful it still needs to be upheld. I may say to them: "I will not stand to be lied to, this is a deal breaker. If you go out for dinner with a friend and that is why you are late, tell me. If you leave the house an hour early because you need some time alone, tell me. With this, I promise to do the same in my communication with you."

Create a habit of thinking of your boundaries when you enter into new relationships of any sort. Be mindful of your communication of them. Remember you are not creating barriers, topics of non-conversation which you hide behind, you are setting boundaries which open up honest, vulnerable, and transparent communication which allows trust and respect to flourish.

Humans and horses differ in the way they communicate. Horses are black and white, and most humans tend to be stuck in the gray. When a horse communicates with another horse, there is no question of what is being communicated. They give subtle cues at first and will become more assertive in their approach until the other horse gets the message.

As previously stated, horses learn from the release of pressure. When they communicate with each other, the pressure is never confusing, and they never release the pressure at the wrong time. As humans we tend to avoid setting clear boundaries, and whether with our horses or other humans, we blur lines and confuse expectations.

Consistency is key. To be consistent in our communication with others, we must be consistent with ourselves. I find I need to take time to really think about what is bothering me in an upsetting situation because when I allow my mind to go on autopilot, I tend to send conflicting messages.

When I catch myself in this state, I have to sort out my feelings independently before I decide to bring them to the other person. If I am confused, they will be even more so, and I will not be able to communicate clearly. At this point for me it helps to speak with an empathetic friend, one who is non-judgmental and allows me to vocalize my feelings and confusion, and in return to have a rational and compassionate sounding board. You will figure out, or maybe you already know, how you best process your thoughts and feelings. Some do it best with paper and pen, some through forms of meditation, and some through conversation. I tend to use a combination of all three. The important part is that I am able to process clearly how I feel and why, and how I can clearly and effectively communicate it if needed.

CHAPTER FOUR

Emotional State of Mind

"Frustration ends where knowledge begins."

Clinton Anderson

The concept discussed in this chapter is among one of the most important topics in this book.

Let's talk about emotions. We all feel emotions, and our emotions can directly affect how we are perceived, how we communicate, and the results of our communication. Throughout this chapter, I will mostly focus on frustration. However, I think it is essential to talk about the importance of practicing mindfulness regarding all of our emotions first.

I always found the situations that set me back the most were those where someone would excuse their inappropriate behavior because they believed they had no control over how they felt. In reality, they were saying they had no control over how they reacted when certain feelings arose. We hear things like, "Oh don't worry about them, they are just having a bad day, they didn't mean that." We have heard "Sorry about that. They get like that when they are mad." Or how about in schools where students told me that they "could not" or "would not" do particular things because someone else just made them mad.

Emotions are meant to be felt, they are part of our human experience, they teach us how to feel empathy and live a compassionate life, but they should not be used as excuses to treat others poorly, stop us from accepting personal responsibility, or hinder our growth.

We may not be able to control emotions that are triggered in us, but we certainly can learn to control how we react, and the decisions we make once emotions are felt. Sudden onset of emotion should serve as an opportunity to practice mindful responses and conscious communication and to dig deeper and reflect on the causes of our reaction.

While reading further on this subject, I came across a line that I believe is the essence of this chapter. Marc Bekoff, the author of *The Emotional Lives of Animals: A Leading Scientist Explores Animal Joy, Sorrow, and Empathy—and Why They Matter*, wrote *"Although most emotional responses are unconsciously generated—they occur without thinking—we learn to try to think before acting. Thinking allows us to make connections between feelings and actions, and this allows for variability and flexibility in our behavior so that, depending on the social situation, we always do the right thing."*[17]

I think when we work with animals, especially horses, where we create such intimate connections teaches this lesson well and continually offers us opportunities for personal reflection and improvement.

The emotional life of the horse, and many other animals, is often overlooked in our handling and training of them, yet, *"It's because animals have emotions that we're so drawn to them; lacking a shared language, emotions are perhaps our most effective means of cross-species communication. We can share our emotions, we can understand the language of feelings, and that's why we form deep and enduring social bonds with many other beings."*[18] Emotions are the catalyst to deep connections, but emotional reactions are the catalyst to disconnection.

The most destructive emotion I see with people and horses is frustration. Frustration often leads to other emotions that result in actions and reactions we may not be proud of. Frustration often results in anger. Frustration can lead to feeling overwhelmed. Frustration tends to lead to feelings of defeat and results in a person giving up or taking no action at all.

It is not until we recognize where our frustrations come from that we can be mindful enough to prevent them or to work through them successfully. We feel frustrated when we are unsure of how to fix a problem, whether that be dealing with how someone treats us, why someone is driving so slow in front of us, or why our horse or husband won't *just* do what we say.

When we lack knowledge, we become emotional and reactive. There is very little room for mindful thought or conversation in a state of frustration. When we are in the grips of frustration we want to seek the quick and convenient answer like: "That person is just an asshole," or "That driver is an idiot and doesn't know how to drive," or "My horse is just trying to piss me off." These answers do not look to be solved because it is no longer our problem to solve. It is someone else's fault. When we are set to place blame, it is impossible to see the situation from a new and less defensive perspective such as: "That guy must be having a tough day," or

"Wow, that guy is lucky he missed that car, he must not have seen him," or "My horse keeps offering me an answer I am not looking for, I will try teaching him in a way he better understands."

With horses, the best way to eliminate frustration is to learn to speak their language. Horses seek leadership, and we are lucky that they accept us as their leaders because this allows amazing things to happen with horses and humans. We impose our relationship on them, and because of this, it is up to us to learn how they communicate and adjust ourselves accordingly. Knowledge is power. When we learn how to interact with our horses effectively, we create a relationship that is like no other. It is simply magical to feel and see. People are no different. We have the potential to gain knowledge and minimize daily frustrations which result from poor communication.

We assume that because we are all human that we all communicate the same way. This is what gets us into trouble. We all have different communication styles, and it is when we understand that we don't all communicate the exact same way that we have the ability to maintain happy and healthy relationships. Miscommunications are one of the biggest stresses within all relationships and this can all be changed when we learn that not everyone communicates as we do and we learn how to best communicate, despite the differences in communication styles.

According to Sherrie Bourg Carter, Psy.D., author of *High Octane Women*, communication styles vary in many ways. I am going to focus on the styles she describes as *"Competitive versus Affiliative"* and *"Direct versus Indirect"* because I have found them to be accurate to what I observe in people and these styles have offered me a lot of personal insight.[19] I will briefly explain these concepts to help you better understand yourself, the way you prefer to communicate, as well as how those around you communicate, and why you may communicate well or poorly together. I encourage you to take time to self-assess when given a choice. How do you prefer to make decisions?

"Competitive versus Affiliative"

Carter proclaims that individuals who prefer to communicate in the affiliative style communicate in a collaborative style. They tend to like to involve others in their decision making, and they feel as though they need to ask others' opinions before they reach a final decision. When a decision needs to be made for this style of communicator, they are likely to consult their partner, family, or friends in their decision-making process. When an individual who communicates in this way is directly challenged or disagreed with, they tend to interpret that as an aggressive or personal response.

These people differ from those who communicate in a competitive style. Someone of the competitive style communicates with the goals of power, dominance, and competition. When they find themselves in a situation which requires them to make a decision, they tend to rely more on themselves than others and do not require much, if any, input. When communicating the people who speak in a competitive style have a tendency to be more direct, assertive, and challenging.

Which style of communicator describes you best? Interestingly enough I personally find myself having attributes of both, although certainly weigh heavier on the competitive side. I assert my opinions freely. When someone disagrees, however, I try my best to do so in as respectful of a way possible. Nonetheless, sometimes people only perceive the assertion rather than the effort of doing so softly, or as softly as I am able to achieve at that moment. Remember we are all a work in progress, right? I also make decisions pretty easily without the opinions of others. I will speak about them after they are made and tend to feel as though someone is challenging me when they do not agree. I have had to be very mindful to overcome getting defensive or reactive in these situations. I do not always succeed but I am aware of it, and that is progress. By recognizing where I fall when communicating stylistically, I can see why I clash with some people in my life more than others.

"Direct versus Indirect"

According to Carter, direct or indirect styles of communicating refer to how we communicate when we need something done. We all know people who communicate directly and when they do there is less chance of their needs being misunderstood. There is, however, a risk the person they are speaking to may take offense to their directness. We often refer to these people as blunt; they come right out and say what they need, want, and feel.

When we communicate in an indirect style there is a higher chance of misunderstanding, yet a smaller chance of offending the person we are communicating with. Although some people clearly lean toward one style more than the other on a regular basis, we have a tendency to use both forms on occasion. In either case, when individuals with two different styles come together in conversation, it causes a greater risk of tension and stress in the relationship.

Carter asserts that relationships among people who differ in communication are not doomed. She highlights, *"In fact, it's often our differences that make us interesting, even attracted to another person. The keys to making differences work are understanding and flexibility."*[20] To work together despite our different communication styles, we must be understanding and flexible; these go hand in hand with empathetic and mindful or conscious. Remember, *"Frustration starts where knowledge ends."*

Here you are gaining knowledge to help alleviate your frustrations. When you start to become frustrated in your relationships, begin looking for answers rather than for blame. Discovering your communication style versus those around you is a great place to begin.

I have witnessed that the communication style of the horse handler can be what makes or breaks a partnership with their horse, or it can stand in the way of them reaching their full potential. When handling horses, we need to learn to be more direct in our communication skills. It is when we do this that we can set clear goals and communicate with them in a way that creates trust and respect and will best get us the results we desire.

Understanding and flexibility are what allow direct communication to be soft and effective at the same time. It is this very concept that needs to be applied to our relationships with people as well as horses. Learning is key and based on the fact that you have read this book through to now you likely value educating yourself. Better understanding brings about personal awareness but doesn't mean you should expect perfection from now on. It means you will be better, little by little, one aware moment at a time.

Our understanding of communication, especially how others perceive our style of communication, allows us to become more flexible in our approach to others. As a result of our self-awareness and flexibility, we can make small changes in our communication. Our communication should still be a reflection of our authentic self. We do not need to change our personality. Rather we may play with our approach to people by being a little more assertive with some who take advantage, or a little softer toward those who find we are too rigid. These changes will be subtle, yet likely will be noticed for good or for bad.

If we begin to assert ourselves with someone who we usually allow to push past our boundaries, it is a great opportunity to have an open conversation about what you have learned and why you have decided to change your communication with them.

Remember, boundaries open conversation. We cannot allow ourselves to place barriers and create more conflict by arming ourselves rather than protecting ourselves.

I want to take this time to write about the importance of communication within our romantic relationships. I suggest reading *The Five Love Languages* by Gary Chapman. I will go over his concepts briefly, however, to be able to understand and utilize this information to the best of your ability you should read his book. Chapman teaches us that there are five ways that we speak and understand emotional love. He states that we all receive love differently, just as we need to recognize that our horses receive love very differently than humans when we work with them, we must understand that our partner may receive love differently than we do. If we only offer them love in the way we need it, we will be left feeling like we are on completely different pages. It is important to be flexible in offering others love in the ways they need it in order to maintain healthy and happy relationships.

Chapman believes the five love languages to be:

"Words of Affirmation"
Here, he explains the power of spoken word. Understanding the power of verbal affirmation with our partner is invaluable. *"Verbal compliments, or words of appreciation, are powerful communicators of love."*[21]

This is not about feeding our partner's ego. We need to feel appreciated, and words of affirmation do just that. When we become more mindful in our communication with others—especially our loved ones—we will begin to see what we appreciate more clearly. Rather than simply think about it, express it. There are many ways you can offer words of affirmation; they can be verbal, through a small written note, a text, or whatever you think is suitable to express your appreciation through the use of words.

Personally, I know this is a need of mine within a romantic

relationship. I need to feel as though my partner is proud of me and appreciates my hard work. When I do not feel this way, I begin to feel frustration and resentment build up, and those emotions have a tendency to come out in snappy comments that seem as though they come "out of nowhere" to my partner. Through practicing mindful communication, I have discovered that I can communicate this need more effectively. It has also allowed me time to reflect on when and why I begin to feel negatively toward my partner at these times.

"Quality Time"

Quality time is different for everyone due to our varying interests and values. Chapman asserts that when using the term "quality time," he means "*giving someone your undivided attention. I don't mean sitting on a couch watching television together.*"[22] He speaks of the importance of face-to-face conversation where we make eye contact and show our partner their importance through distraction-free communication.

Quality time is important to me in a relationship. Although I have come to realize that it does not hold the same value for me as others. I need quality time, yet I also greatly appreciate our time where we can be together doing other things. As a teacher, I used to interact with a very large number of people daily and needed quiet time to turn down after my day. It is here that I have discovered one of the ways my husband and I differ. I appreciate our *quiet* time together and he needs *quality* time together at the end of his day. This is something that he and I both know and understand now. It takes some work to ensure we are both having our needs met without making the other feel like they are not a priority.

"Receiving Gifts"

A gift, something tangible that we can hold, feel, or see, is often perceived as "*visible symbols of love*" and hold very high value for many, as affirmed by Chapman.[23] When we get a gift that we can hold, we interpret that as an affirmation that our loved one was thinking of us when we were absent. The gift represents the thought and giving the gift is an expression of love, according to Chapman.

Not everyone sees the same importance in receiving gifts, just as we don't all value words of affirmation in the same way. If you do have a partner who feels loved by gifts, it is something you can easily hone in on and use. This does not mean you must continually spend money on your partner; it may be a flower you picked that was their favorite color. It is the tangible thing that shows that you know them and that you thought of them in their absence.

Neither my husband nor I need to receive love in this way; although it is appreciated when it is done, it is not something which brings about tension or frustration on either of our part when it is not done. That being said, the items he has bought for me which show how well he knows me hold significant importance to me and I cherish them.

"Acts of Service"

Chapman tells his readers that when acts of service, anything we know our partner would appreciate us doing, are done in a positive manner they are expressions of love. People perceive acts of service as expressions of love because of the effort and meaning behind them. It is worth noting that you must first know your partner well enough to know what they would like you to do without being asked, whether that be the laundry, house cleaning, a chore, or an errand. The other aspect of this is doing it to the degree they believe it to be done right. When we understand what our partner likes having done and to what extent it shows attentiveness and appreciation.

For example, if your partner is always the one to do the laundry and you never see it unfolded in a heap in the basket, rather it is neatly placed in drawers designated to specific items, it is important to recognize these things prior to taking on the task. If you decide to do the laundry as your act of service and you hastily fold them and put them away in any old drawer, you will not be sending a complete message of love. Your partner may appreciate that you "tried", but they may also feel slightly resentful or unappreciated as they re-fold and rearrange all of the clothing. They may even say, "I would rather do it right myself than have you do it and me have to go and fix it." It is important that we get to know our partners well enough that our acts of service do not add to conflict. They are an act of love and in this case *"actions speak louder than words."*

I have come to realize that my husband receives love in this way. It is important for me to remember to complete my acts to his standard of completion when I do. Not because he will be upset or angry with me if I don't, rather it will be through my attention to detail that he will feel the most love. In this case, a lack of attention to detail to him is interpreted as a lack of care. It is a waste of an act of service if that is how he is left feeling in the end.

"Physical Touch"

Physical touch is a powerful way to communicate love. *"For some individuals, physical touch is their primary love language. Without it, they feel unloved,"* Chapman explains.[24] Physical touch varies from an embrace to a touch of a hand as you pass your partner in the hall. It is also important to recognize and learn the type of physical contact your partner enjoys and to make sure that your efforts are meeting their needs. Some people enjoy a soft or subtle touch as it communicates affection to them whereas others enjoy a passionate kiss. Offering a balance of physical touch with some partners is important. I have learned from personal experience and from conversations with others that if the only physical touch offered is perceived as sexual then they may become resentful of that touch because they lack the type of touch that makes them feel appreciated rather than just wanted.

The balance of physical touch can be difficult within relationships because the perception of the purpose of physical touch is so important. When one's first love language is physical touch, this is likely not going to be as big of a concern; they will feel loved through all or many forms. If physical touch is not your partner's first love language, in fact maybe it is their last, then you must be cognizant of the message you are sending them, so you know it makes them feel loved.

Chapman shows the complexity of human nature and communication through the breakdown of how people receive and interpret love differently. Do not allow this to make you feel overwhelmed. Use this as a door to better your communication and relationship. Open the conversation up with your partner and get to know how they receive love the best and what messages you send when you offer love in specific ways.

When our communication breaks down as a result of a number of factors, the best way to begin to fix it is to find our responsibility in it. Yes, some "fault" may be on the other counterpart, such as their own overreaction or something else which makes communication difficult. However, blaming others takes away our power. When we simply look to blame, we will fall into a victim mentality and will not look for solutions, just revenge or justice.

I see this often when working with people and their horses, and honestly, have experienced this personally with horses and in personal relationships. Horses tend to get blamed for their response. The handler or rider seeks to blame and reprimand versus looking for a problem with their own communication. We need to reclaim our power and take responsibility. When we do this we open doors to create better relationships rather than close doors on relationships that could have been successful had we changed our communication even slightly.

Accepting personal responsibility takes away our defensive nature and allows us to set frustration aside. When we stop blaming and start accepting our responsibility we give relationships a chance to not only survive but thrive. Even relationships we were sure would "never work." Frustration ends all constructive communication. Replace frustration with vulnerable and self-reflective conversation, and you will be surprised where it takes you.

I'm going to offer you an example that I hope shows you how we limit ourselves and our relationships when we do not know how to communicate in a way that will bring them to their truest potential:

As I have mentioned, I grew up riding horses. I began when I was seven years old, and I learned from some amazing people. However, I now know that I never really learned how to approach the issues I was having with my horses from a communication perspective. If my horse was scared of specific objects and obstacles, things above her head, for example, I would use that as an excuse to avoid them. I avoided problem areas with her like the plague. I did not help her with the problem. I simply blamed her for the fact that we couldn't do some of the same things and activities others could do with their horses because I had a spooky horse, not because I had not shown her how to cope with her fears. She was the problem, not me.

When social media became more popular the horse world opened up to me in a whole new way. I watched a video of a gentleman lay his horse down in a fan-filled stadium. Then he proceeded to cover the horse with a giant tarp. This blew my mind! *How could he do that when I could barely accept a ribbon at a standstill on a windless day!?* I first thought how lucky he was to have such a quiet horse. Then I saw more videos like this. I went to watch a colt starting competition called *Road to the Horse,* and I saw similar things in person with lots of different horses. It was then that I finally took personal responsibility for my relationship with my horses in the past for having reached a limited potential.

I grew up having no idea what horses and humans were truly capable of when they communicated clearly. Now that I know, I don't lay my horse under tarps. I do, however, see our potential as boundless and I look at breakdowns in communication as opportunities to open new doors rather than excuses which limit growth.

I believe that human relationships are the same. Until we can see how we are part of the problem and the solution we will never see the true potential of our relationship, and we will eventually come to a standstill, feeling the need to move on. Had we known what clear communication could bring to us, that very relationship could have been one that was inspiring rather than frustrating. When we learn our own language and the language of those around us, we begin to communicate with fewer misunderstandings. When misunderstandings or miscommunications happen the conflict will not escalate, rather it will turn into an open conversation which quickly moves us forward. Keep in mind here, not every relationship has the same potential. Just because you are capable of mindful communication does not mean the other person will be receptive. This is not a reflection of us, rather a circumstance beyond our control. Where we gain our control back here, is in the opportunity to recognize the limits of the relationship. Appreciate the person for what they can offer us, but we need not convince ourselves that we can change them. That is not our responsibility; it is theirs.

It is important to note becoming mindful in our communication will not prevent us from falling into conflict ever again, rather it will give us the insight we need to get to the other side of a conflict with our values, emotions, and confidence still intact. Hopefully and more than likely, you will also come to the other side of the conflict with the relationship less scathed then in the past.

Exercise:

Revisit this chapter when you have your journal and some time. Reflect on yourself and determine how you communicate with others and how it affects your relationships. Then take the time to discover how you like to receive love, place them in order from highest to lowest and plan to set a goal to make time to communicate these to your partner clearly, and offering them time to express how they best receive love as well.

Lastly, write out three things you intend to do today to show your partner love the way they need it most. I suggest making this list of ways to show your partner love each day part of your morning journaling routine.

Some ideas could be:

- Tell them something you are most proud of them for.

- Write them a note and place it somewhere they will unexpectedly find it.

- Get out of bed earlier than needed to offer them a hug and kiss before they leave for work.

- Check off an item on their list that you know you can complete to their satisfaction.

- Buy them a shirt that you think will look great on them, or take that further by arranging a dinner date for you both and ask them to wear the shirt then.

Once again, I recommend reading *The Five Love Languages* by Gary Chapman to gain the most from his research and expertise.

CHAPTER FIVE

This is Not For Me

*"Knowledge is knowing that a tomato is a fruit,
wisdom is not putting it in a fruit salad."*

Miles Kington

With horses and people, our ego tends to rule our commitment to them. Often when we hear the word ego in connection to someone we think of someone who thinks very highly of themselves. This is likely due to the use of the term egotistical. Someone who has allowed their ego to be in charge of their thoughts and actions is, however, not always the one who is coming across as conceited or self-centered.

The ego is the "I." The inner voice, that compares us to others and feeds unhealthy thinking and behavioral patterns. Sometimes our ego boosts us so high that we are selfish and self-centered. It often, however, does the opposite. Our ego wants to keep us safe and is always looking to keep us in check, so much so in comparison to others that we never feel good enough. We limit risk-taking, and we live a less fulfilling life than we deserve. Ego is interesting because when we allow it to be in control, it means we give our thoughts so much power that we are unable to make decisions in our best interest. I have seen this with people in regard to their horse, their lover, brother, sister, friend, business partner— you get the point.

A fundamental lesson in life is to recognize when something is unhealthy for us. If we do not look out for ourselves, acknowledge and act on these situations, then we will live a life conflicted with what we know is right for us in our heart and what our ego is telling us is safe for us. If we learn to listen to our intuition rather than our ego, we will discover that we have all of the answers to our "Should I?" questions in the least self-destructive way possible.

Remaining in an unhealthy relationship is often one of the ways we allow our ego to take control of our decision making. We allow our ego to tell us that it is our fault things aren't working or that we can fix the other person. This can be the case with education, therapy, or personal growth in one form or another, and often things can be made successful. However, sometimes it doesn't need to be fixed. It needs to be left behind or placed in the hands of someone better suited. *Not better. Just better suited.*

When the wrong horse and rider combination come together, it can be dangerous. It can be equally, if not more dangerous, for a wrong combination of people to force a relationship. It is important that we understand that sometimes walking away from something or someone requires more strength than holding on.

This can be quite difficult with horses because we invest time, money, and emotion into them. They are hard to let go of, but we must recognize that just because the relationship is not working for us does not mean it won't work for someone else. It is not an insult, even if our ego tells us otherwise.

I am very fortunate to work with my husband in our horse business because we both know and appreciate each other's strengths and we use them to our advantage. There have been a few times when a client has handed me a horse because of a behavioral issue, and I have told them, "This is not a horse for me right now. This is a Mike horse." I have come to recognize that my ego is the thing that will get me hurt or have me miscommunicate with a horse and achieve poor results.

I have discovered that since having our daughter, my self-preservation instinct is much stronger than it used to be. I have found that I step back when I know I should step forward or I question my methods. I am learning how to teach horses with intimidating behaviors, such as kicking, at a distance which allows me success. In the past, and maybe sometime again in the future, when a horse showed aggressive behavior toward its handler I knew that it was not a horse that I would get through to any better than the unsure owner, even if I have more informed timing or an educated approach. Part of my knowledgeable approach is knowing when I am not right for the job. A horse that is showing excessively intimidating behaviors requires a handler who shows confidence and perseverance at all times to get through the situation. As I learned from horsewoman Andrea Anderson, we cannot get pulled into their drama. This is something I am learning to control. Unfortunately, it does not come naturally to me. We will discuss this later in the book.

Despite my want to be independent and work with each horse handed to me, I ask for help when I begin to question myself. My husband steps in and with incredible timing and unwavering confidence handles the situation. I step back in on the training of the horse when it has reached a level of understanding that I know I can confidently work with. I handle horses that come my way confidently the majority of the time. That being said, there is a small percentage of horses brought to us that I am not the right person for in the beginning stages of their training, and that is okay. A very small percent of the time they are simply never going to be for me, and that too is okay. I have used this same mentality with relationships. If a person is not right for me romantically, friend-wise, or business-wise, that does not make them bad. It just means they are not healthy for me and I have to keep moving forward. It also means that I will still be kind to them. My serious efforts though will shift to those who make me feel alive and happy. We have to remember we are not going to be everyone's cup of tea and not everyone will be ours. That is not mean, it is the truth.

We have to be able to recognize when a situation or relationship is not for us, and this comes with some pretty serious personal research that is absolutely necessary. Sometimes all we need is a little help, and we are on our way. Sometimes, we need to know when it simply does not suit our needs, or we do not suit their needs. A lack of compatibility may occur in relationships due to the couple's differing love languages, friends' communication styles which drastically clash, or some other reasons such as different values, beliefs, or boundaries. Maybe, you cannot stay in the same place as someone emotionally, you want growth and they want familiarity, and that is okay. We need to silence the ego when it tells us we have to fix things or we have to hold onto things. It is not true in every case. Everything is not meant to work for us, and when it works for someone else down the road, it is not a reflection of our failure, rather a reflection of our right choice.

So, how do you know when to let go?

When my husband Mike and I first started dating, he said something profound. I'm sure he didn't know just how profound it really was at the time. He said to me, "We will know we are not working when the bad days outweigh the good days."

What if we applied this to everything in our life? We can apply this to work, marriages, friendships, sports, hobbies, anything we do that should leave us feeling positive, and instead is leaving us feeling negative. Unless it is something like bringing up your child through the terrible twos or obnoxious teens. Those things we can't walk away from may just need a good glass of wine and a bubble bath, walk, phone date, or whatever will help us every once in a while to cope. We should be able to eliminate or change the circumstance to become less negative or damaging in most situations.

There are many ways we can change our circumstances when we begin to notice our bad days are outweighing our good days. Sometimes it is difficult to narrow down our bad days to just one thing. Maybe we are feeling down, sluggish, annoyed, impatient, etc. Whatever it is the fact remains, we know we do not feel happy.

I personally have made some changes recently that had a major impact on my perspective. My changes made me go from feeling like all of my problems and unhappiness were just me, that I was feeling down for no reason, to discovering a reason and making a major life change to fix it.

My husband and I had been living a lifestyle that had us burning the candle at both ends over the last few years. I was finding myself getting low on energy, drive, and patience on a daily basis. In preparation for our wedding, I made a change to my routine and overall lifestyle. I decided to start taking time for myself by prioritizing healthy eating and exercise because I had an end goal which was to feel the best I could in my own body as I stepped into my wedding dress on one of the most important days of my life. With the support of a great group of friends, one in particular who met me at home at 5:30 a.m. for 60 days to work out, I began to feel great.

Interestingly, even though I physically changed and was visibly more in shape, I received more compliments within the first two weeks of my 60-day overhaul than I did at the end. The compliments were less about weight and more about *energy*. I had colleagues and students stopping and asking what I was doing differently. I even heard the line we all love, "You're glowing!" Now, to be honest, I attributed this to the hard work I was doing at the time, but it was important I did because it was a tremendous external motivator to keep going, and it was exactly what I needed to hear.

Fast forward to seven months past the wedding. Winter had sufficiently set into my mind, the cold season had taken over my house, and I was feeling the full effects of my best friend moving thousands of miles away. Again, I felt like I was searching for the energy to do the little things in my daily life. Some days, conversation was a struggle. I don't think I was depressed, but I certainly was not feeling like life was fantastic, and I should have been because it was and is. My ego gave me the lecture of "*why can't you just be happy, look at what you have, you are impossible to please, you are the problem, not your circumstance,*" and so on. How I was feeling was reflected in my work, my marriage, and my parenting. I knew I needed to make a change. I needed to change my routine and my personal awareness, similarly to when I was getting in shape for the wedding, although I had *no* desire to do what I had done. There are a couple of reasons for this, I was feeling good about myself as far as my physical health, and I knew I did not have the mental energy to push myself and maintain what I had done before due to my work schedule.

Instead of an extensive exercise routine and strict meal planning to help me, I started focusing on what I needed mentally to regain energy. I began reading more, and I don't mean romance novels that allowed me to step out of my world and into someone else's, although I do see value in those too. I read to learn, to know, and to discover more about things that interested me and made me appreciate life. Then I started connecting with like-minded women and began surrounding myself with positive energy. I began focusing on what I really wanted and what I love and desire. I began to practice daily gratitude, and once again I changed my routine, very much like when I was doing my exercise program. I started to get up early and start my day in a way that I enjoyed. Rather than work out, this time for me that meant a good tea, writing, lavender oil, and soft lighting.

About a week into my new morning routine I saw the same change in how others perceived me as I did when I began eating better and exercising the winter before. I heard the term "glowing" again in reference to how I looked. I had people comment on the change in my energy. To top it off, I had a grade nine student tell me that she enjoyed coming to my class because it was "peaceful."

Life can be heavy if we don't take the time to take care of ourselves, focus some energy inward, and fuel our bodies with love. For me, part of this process had been reflecting on what drained me and how I could make changes to set my soul on fire, and I did just that.

Through my new mental clarity and practices, I began to get to know myself better. I gave myself the space to think about my life, what I enjoyed, and what I didn't enjoy rather than just floating through from day to day knowing something was off, yet never being brave enough to confront my own thoughts.

I discovered, much to my dread of judgment and disappointing others, that I had fallen out of love with my career. It took a lot of soul searching to realize that the thing that I had worked tirelessly to become was now not what I wanted to be; a teacher, or at least not a classroom teacher. As I really allowed myself to think and feel, I learned that I felt like I was teaching the wrong people, or maybe it was just the wrong environment. I will always teach, but not in that exact capacity.

One day I began to write in my journal about how I had been feeling for the last few years, and this is what came flooding out:

Guilt can transfix us, or it can raise us to change.

Over the last nine years, a lot of the mix of anxiety and excitement had worn off within the routines of my teaching career. I had learned to relax within the confines of being a teacher. That being said, this shift from new and anxious to confident and assured showed me something pivotal which eventually brought me to walking away from my classroom.

Without the feelings of a new job, the excitement it brought, and with the found courage to work through almost any situation I encountered in my early days as a teacher, my energy source was gone. Over the last six or so years I had been stealing from my banked energy. I consider my banked or built up energy to have come from the spark of excitement and uncertainty that I felt in myself so often in those first few years. It was as though all the new things, the tasks I felt challenged by, ignited an energy that sustained me for quite some time.

Since then, however, I had noticed the drain that was my career. My reserve of energy had been depleting due to a number of factors in my life, and my career choice had been the most draining. I was a new wife; we had been married for less than a year. I was the mother of a busy three-year-old, who I first left in the care of someone else to return to work at the age of four months. She was so tiny and so innocent. The nature of my career made being away from work difficult. It was then that I truly experienced deep-seated and emotionally shattering guilt for the first time.

I had felt guilt in little waves throughout life up to that point; I forgot to return my library book and found it after I had moved, I lied to my mom, I kissed a boy I was told to stay away from, I forgot to feed the dog, the list goes on. You know, those little bobbles that make you have an upset feeling in your stomach that makes you pay a little closer attention next time or not procrastinate when asked to do something important. No, this guilt was nothing like a sick feeling in my stomach as a motivator to do the right thing. It was an emotional waterfall that rushed from my head to my toes that shook me to my core.

I had been warned when I was pregnant about what some moms refer to as "mom guilt." I began experiencing this as soon as I found out I was pregnant. To hear others acknowledge it made me feel less unhinged; however, it did not make it stop. Although I had been warned and felt better knowing I was not alone, it still did not prepare me for the gravity with which the guilt would consume me. In fact, the only thing I found that helped it in the last three years was when I decided to start taking care of myself mentally, emotionally, and physically. You would think that focusing more on my own well-being would do the opposite, that I would feel guilty for prioritizing my needs, yet it didn't. I began to feel more in control, I was regaining energy, and I was able to see that changes clearly needed to be made.

Guilt was consuming my inner world. While on maternity leave my substitutes, yes multiple, had a difficult time with the students on my class lists. Guilt. When I returned to work my daughter was being rocked to sleep by someone else. Guilt. My time to mark and plan lessons interrupted the little time I had with my only baby. Guilt. My husband got what was left of me at the end of a long and emotionally draining day. There was nothing left for him. Guilt. I had been so focused on my new normal I had forgotten important things, like calling my family. Guilt.

The guilt did not stop after I got into my new routine as I was reassured would happen by so many. I had a baby who slept delightfully well, bringing with it its own guilt as I spoke to new mom friends struggling night and day to get their baby to stop crying and just go to sleep. Although she was a "good" baby, she still required so much of me—every day, more and more. With every passing day, she slept a little less and needed ever-changing attention. As if that was not enough, with tears being shed in the morning and often as I laid her down to sleep at night, I also had responsibilities to help my soon-to-be husband care for our abundance of animals, what I refer to as our "fur-children."

As our home life blossomed, so did our horse business, and so did the guilt. I felt guilty for not riding my horse, not helping with chores, and without my husband quite understanding the pressure, self-induced and not, I received subtle and not so subtle jabs about my absence from the barn. He wasn't doing it to be mean or make me feel worse. I felt that he did not understand how difficult it was to be feeling like I was only able to give 25% of my effort and time to multiple things I expected myself to be able to put 100% into.

The time outside my classroom began to fill with more work and my ability to say no was non-existent. With every "yes" I felt guilty, but I knew the guilt of a "no" would be even more damaging. I felt, within my heart, that I was failing in every aspect of my life. As someone with high personal expectations, maybe due to being a teacher as well, failing was tearing me apart.

As with every career, maybe more so in public service jobs, the expectation to give my all was put upon me by myself and also by the ever-critical and scrutinizing public. I was not arriving to work early as I had in my first few years. I felt like I was barely able to get there at all. I was arriving on time, yet that was not good enough in my eyes. I felt it was not good enough in the eyes of many other teachers I passed as I felt their judging glares as I hurried by them, tea and keys in hand. My mind was so convinced I was doing wrong that it convinced me others thought the same. I knew they had been there long before me and I was sure they felt that I was not holding up to their standard as a competent colleague. I am not sure if they were actually judging me at the time or if I was so frustrated with myself that my ego was doing a great job of making it seem like everyone else noticed I was a failure as well. If they were judging me, I do not blame them. Early on in my career I likely judged some other teacher who I thought was arriving "too late" or leaving "too early" with no regard for their life beyond the classroom. This is very common in the teaching profession, and I believe even teachers tend to make this mistake, thinking that when you become a "teacher," that is it and that title defines you entirely.

No one close to me thought I was failing. They all thought I was doing "what was best" and doing a good job at it. Or so I was told. But I felt weighted. In my mind, I was a disappointment, to the true definition of the word. I was feeling deep sadness and displeasure caused by the non-fulfillment of my hopes and expectations of myself.

I was overwhelmed with life. My personal responsibility was to make a change to allow myself to grow and offer as much to myself as I do others. To do this, I had to find the light I lost. When I began to make small changes to my daily practices, I felt my guilt shift inside me. I had moments of personal reassurance telling myself that I would get control and I would not always feel this way. One day I had the thought that I should leave teaching. I let it sit in my mind for a while before I allowed it to escape past my lips.

Let me talk about guilt! Wow, I felt it rush over me as if to put me back in my place. How dare I walk away from something "so good." I worked hard to get to where I was, and I had a lot of help along the way from emotional and financial support from my parents to job opportunities placed practically in my lap. I had benefits, security, and summers off. How could someone think they should leave a job where they have summers off? I allowed myself to work through these thoughts and combat them with the truth. I discovered that I already knew none of that was important.

I began slowly telling people that I was making a change and for the most part, I was met with amazing positivity. I could feel the old and inspired self I once knew surfacing at times, and as I became married to the idea of leaving my full-time teaching position, I had more of these moments and began to feel more inspired to create change.

I found myself removing the title "classroom teacher" from my shoulders like a heavy blanket. I was slowly sliding it off, one shoulder at a time, and with every movement from under this blanket, I was acknowledging the weight that was being lifted. I had met and taught beside many beautiful souls who had wanted nothing more than to teach, and then who later slipped away into new careers without a sound, due to many reasons, but I saw mostly that their expectation and their reality of being a teacher were very different. I had it very easy in comparison to some of those teachers.

I was not feeling out of control in my workplace, rather out of control of my life. However, my job played a large part in that. Maybe that was partly why I didn't seem to fit anymore. I was not willing to have "teacher" be my defining role in life, or at least not in same the way it was at the time.

This is no insult to those who solely define themselves as a classroom teacher; they are what holds our education system together and they help create a future for our world. When I see teachers who *love* their job, I am so grateful for them. Teachers should love their job, just as everyone else should love theirs.

I really enjoy teaching; I think this needs to be made very clear. I love the shift in someone's energy when they learn something new that they want to learn. There is something magical about it, and whenever I see it, I am reminded why I am meant to teach. I love opening doors for people and helping shift perspectives and perceptions. I feel aligned when I am able to light a spark of curiosity in someone that lead them down paths they may not have taken otherwise.

So then I thought of my defining roles. I am a mother, a wife, a sister, a daughter, a horsewoman, an empowerer, a creative mind, and a life-long learner. I am all these things and more. I will forever be a teacher; I am rewriting my curriculum.

I recently began a journey that brought me back to this very chapter to add in my newest enlightenment. My goal was always to complete my master's degree. It wasn't until I left teaching that I discovered why getting my master's degree in education was not for me, and how I learned that I needed to master something else.

The very first year I taught, I worked day and night to learn a subject I needed to teach and one that I had struggled with in school personally. I was hired to be a science teacher. The English major who avoided math and sciences like the plague was hired to teach science. Don't get me wrong; we aren't talking grade twelve chemistry here, it was merely grade seven science where we talked about things like geological plate tectonics, time-space, the rock cycle, mixtures and solutions, heat, and the ecosystem. With a real focus and determination to teach and teach well, I managed, but it was not like teaching English where ideas popped into my head in the shower or at night while I was supposed to be sleeping. It took a lot of trying.

Despite being hired into a position I fit somewhat haphazardly into, one that sometimes felt like I had been thrown to the wolves with not much more than a small plate of bacon to deter them temporarily from eating me alive, I set my sights on more. I told myself that by my fifth year of teaching I would complete my master's degree in administration. I felt the calling to lead, and this was the only avenue I saw at that time. I held onto my desire to get my master's for quite a few years, even beyond my fifth year which was my personal deadline, but in the end, the timing seemed off, and my goals seemed to be shifting.

I watched what the leaders of my school were doing, and it just didn't seem to be the type of leadership role that suited my desires. I saw great leaders being defeated by having their hands tied by red tape, not always able to lead in the way I knew they wished they could. I saw them grow weary from trying to lead in a system that wanted to make sure they always knew that in reality they were being led, and were not leading.

I admire those who chose leadership roles within the school system. I think they are a breed of their own and deserve a lot of respect. They are the glue that holds a school together. If you don't believe me, visit a school for a day. You will see what I mean as you either witness it falling apart at the seams, or see one with a strong administrative team where it seems to run like a well-oiled machine. When I picture myself as a leader, however, I do not see myself holding something together, but instead building something up.

I want you to know how much I truly respect the people who take on leadership roles in schools. Those jobs are demanding and often thankless. Let me take this time, even if it doesn't apply to all my readers, to say thank you. If you have ever or continue to lead in any capacity in a school, thank you.

After a number of years and schools, I discovered that getting my master's degree in education was not for me, but mastering in something that fed my desire to lead still was. The path I took that led me into teaching was not wrong. My want to go into administration at that time was not wrong. My shifts in perspective and experiences as a result of these things led me to exactly where I needed to be.

When I was teaching high school, I would be woken up by inspiration in the night. I would think about my plans for my English class all the way to school and rewrite the day I had planned previously. I was compelled to teach lessons with life lessons attached. I wanted to teach my students things that made them really *think* about themselves, their choices, the world and where they stood in it.

My favorite thing to teach in English class was dystopian literature, a form of literature which is used to examine social and political structures. I am not much into politics, but I am really into inspiring critical thinking and personal reflection. This unit allowed both of these perfectly.

One of my favorite short stories to read and teach was *The Ones Who Walk Away from Omelas* by Ursula K. Le Guin. It was a story about a "perfect" world created for everyone to be in bliss. The way Le Guin describes it is beautiful because she tells her reader that this "perfect" world is entirely individual. She only describes activities in the community for the purpose of the story, but essentially asks the reader to picture Omelas as their perfect world. There is a catch, however, in order for the people of Omelas to remain in absolute bliss someone has to suffer.

It is an innocent child who suffers. She describes the child's suffering, and it elicits the perfect emotional response to counteract the joy we felt from creating and living in our dream world.

Each character in the short story learns of the child's suffering at an age where they have already become well accustomed to what true joy and bliss feel like for them and then comes the moral challenge. Some would choose to stay in Omelas. Some would decide they could not live in ignorance of their new knowledge and they would walk away from Omelas and all of their happiness into an unknown world.

I would challenge my students to think about what they would choose. I wanted them to think not only of their ideal world but also their morals. Was their desire for happiness more important than the quality of life for one child? I wanted them to be honest with themselves, and I wanted them to dig deep. I encouraged them to look at the world we live in today, and I asked them to draw comparisons between Le Guin's fictional world and our own.

My goal was not to upset my students. However, it certainly was to stir the emotions and thoughts that made them analyze the world around them and who they are based on their needs, wants, values and beliefs.

For some, the lesson did everything I wanted. It sparked a light of inspiration to discover who they were and what they stood for. For others, it reaffirmed what they already thought they knew of the world and themselves. For some, it was a confusing story with a strange ending that talked about a kid in a closet.

In the final years of my teaching career, the confused students seemed to be the majority in the room. These particular students did not leave my classroom more enlightened in any way. I was seeing more and more students engaging less in critical thinking and falling more into the overwhelm of their everyday life. They seemed so preoccupied with their current situation which, ironically, was them worrying about their past or future so much that they seemed utterly lost in their present. They saw no use in learning what was being presented because if they focused on that, then it required their focus to shift from where they are comfortable.

Through some personal processing, I discovered that teaching that story was a backdoor way of teaching my students things I saw they needed to learn beyond English class. It was then, through teaching that very story at the end of my teaching career that told me that going through the backdoor to teach these students what I knew they needed was not working. I needed to walk up to the front door, not even knock, let myself in, and teach it directly. This was for me! This is what I need to master in; this is where I need to lead.

As I wrote this particular section, my fellow teachers were gathering picket signs and heading out in a massive snowstorm to plead with our government to listen and help better our classrooms. I was not with them. Based on my relationship with myself over the last three years and my constant state of perpetual guilt I should have been feeling waves of it, yet I didn't. I was in my home with lavender oil scent flowing from my diffuser while my daughter sniffled with a cold that I, no doubt, brought home to her from my school. My house was clean, and chores were done so when she asked for a cuddle; I gladly gave it to her. That day, I did not feel guilt.

The next day, I marched with my fellow teachers and proudly supported our cause. I felt a burden lifted as I knew when I stood beside them the following day that while I would be fighting for a better education for my daughter and every other child who deserves it, I would not be fighting my personal battle any longer.

As I sat with my journal and wrote and thought and listened, I discovered the need to create a life that I did not need to take a vacation from as a form of escape. As cliché as that sounds, I should clarify. I want to travel to regenerate and seek reprieve from the everyday, however, I do not want to feel as though I will be running away to forget the stress that awaits me back home. I want to vacation to continue my personal growth and to reconnect myself, but I want to *want* to come home. During my last months of teaching, if I were to take a trip, there would be only one thing I would not miss, and that was teaching.

I feel like people will cringe when they read those words, even though it is my heartfelt truth. I understand that stating this may not win some people over as my fans but I will not sugar coat my truth here. This is my experience. I believe the world needs more uncensored truth, especially where our future generations are concerned. I am not looking to offend anyone, teacher, student, or parent throughout these pages and if I do, I apologize.

Perhaps it is more cringe-worthy to hear from a teacher who does not want to teach because of the nature of the job. It sounds like I do not want to help children or that I am abandoning or insulting the profession in some way; however, that is not the case. I will not miss the hours of planning and marking on my family's time. I will not miss the lack of appreciation from parents and students. I will not miss feeling like I am fighting to make a difference in peoples' lives who don't see why things should be different.

I *will* miss working alongside people passionate to impact our youth and those special moments when I saw that I had made an impact in someone's life. That being said, that is still my mission in life.

For nine years, the number of students who have made me feel like I was inconveniencing them with their own education outweighed the number of students who entered my room looking to absorb information to better their future. I may never have been able to appreciate what it is to teach a truly captivated audience had my husband and I not begun teaching clinics in our horse business. The gratitude flowed from our riders after every clinic through hugs, thank-yous, photographs, praise, and even tears. It was so enlightening to teach people who genuinely wanted to learn. They sought our knowledge and listened intently.

I kept wondering, how do I achieve this in my classroom? That was a mistake. I was comparing apples to oranges. I was comparing teaching a group of people who invested in my knowledge to a group of people, both students and parents, who could see that their government wouldn't even invest in my knowledge by making teachers appear greedy and ungrateful. I know this exists in some classrooms, and I did have some students who bounded in my room ready and enthusiastic to learn the lessons of the day, but they were a minority.

Some teachers reading this may completely disagree with me, and that is perfectly okay. In fact, there must be because there are still teachers who plan to teach until they are forced to retire. I want to remind them that all opinions are formed on personal experience, and this is based on mine. I may not have felt this way in my first few years when I still had the expectation that I would set my students' world on fire by sparking interest in any topic I would teach them. Reality hit hard when all too many lessons were met with sighs as I presented my ideas, and after weeks of work, final assignments were accompanied with a disappointing, "Is this good enough?" as a less than good enough assignment got handed to me.

One particular experience shaped this opinion for me, maybe more than all the others, and it wasn't even my work that was invested in it. I was given the opportunity to see my students from a new perspective and it gave me a great deal to reflect on.

I had a colleague who came into my class to offer support, often taking students who have a difficult time to get some one-on-one help. He and I had taught in the same building for a number of years, and he asked if I would mind if he taught my students for a few days. He had created a unit that he thought would be perfect to engage this particular group, a group of students he knew well; many of which he had known for the last six years in an academic capacity.

The class I had at the time was a challenge, not in the sense that people think of when you say you have a difficult class though. Behaviorally, this class was not too bad. I was not at high risk of being told off; no one was violent or aggressive. This was a group of grade twelve students who had learned the system of doing as little as possible and getting the grade. I had a wide range of abilities in this class, from students who had the ability to excel in school if they applied themselves, to students who had a difficult time to write a basic sentence. Despite the academic differences, the one similarity that the majority of these students had was they had no interest in school and even less interest in English class.

The class was comprised of mostly boys which allowed for the opportunity to teach a full lesson geared directly toward boys who were "non-readers." We are taught throughout our years of teaching that if we designed something specifically for these students, the ones who we are told get missed in the planning process, they will be engaged and we will reach them.

The teacher who asked to teach my students had been working on this lesson plan for quite some time. He put together a lesson that used something he was passionate about outside of school and that he thought would connect well with this particular group of students.

It should have worked. It should have caught their attention. It should have given them something to work on that they enjoyed.

It didn't. I sat at my desk and watched it fail. It felt like I was a fly on the wall watching my own lessons being taught. It felt almost surreal to see what was happening right in front of my eyes. I watched as a full class chose to engage *themselves* in things they perceived as important at the time, their phones, sleep, and inappropriate conversations, rather than allowing themselves to be engaged in what was important for them in the future, be it the next day, year, or post-graduation.

The lesson plan contained everything we thought these boys would enjoy; comics, humor, a little bit of swearing, and even a couple sexual references. Keep in mind this was a grade twelve course; there was nothing offensive or too inappropriate, just racy enough that they should have at least taken notice or even looked up and wonder why the lesson was being taught. They didn't. It was at that moment, as I watched someone else struggle to entertain or educate, whichever term you choose, that I discovered I was fighting a losing battle. I watched as a young male teacher struggled to connect with young male students and I saw why.

Our students now live in a generation of constant entertainment. It is not the constant that is the only problem; it is personalized entertainment. Our children no longer have to watch a TV show they do not like because nothing else is on. They can stream a show they want to see. Our children don't have to wait for a movie they saw in the theater to come out on DVD; they can watch it online. Our children don't even have to sit through commercials. Our children don't have to wait for a friend to return a phone call, they text them, and they can even see when they have read it. Our children don't have to sit at home and awkwardly watch a movie with their parents because they have everything they need to be entertained on their person at all times. They know what they find entertaining, whether it be social media, or a game, or a conversation with a friend over text. Why would they offer their attention to anything else that they would not personally choose to do at that moment?

The thought of cell phone use in the classroom will inevitably come up for some of you here, and rightfully so. In September I would come in strong. I had plans on how to control it. I had labeled baskets for them to put their phones in. I gave lectures and chances and then lectured again.

This wore thin as the months rolled on. It does not take many times of being verbally insulted or disrespected to make one gun-shy. I felt my courage to approach students about cell phones deplete and with it, my anxiety increased. As I witnessed this in my classroom, I thought about the fact that these are 17 and 18-year-old people. They drive cars and work, yet I have to be the cell phone police when they are in a classroom. I resolved to the fact that I would tell them to put them away, that they are not needed for the class, similar to how this other teacher introduced himself to my class, but past that, it was their education and responsibility. Sadly, I guarantee if they showed me they couldn't keep their phone away for the sake of graduating they likely aren't keeping it away for driving, both true and devastating.

I looked upon my class that day, and I said to myself, *this is not for me.* I had discovered that my bad days were outweighing my good days in my job and this influenced how I felt about my life as a whole. It was not my family, my horses, or anything else. It took some honesty with myself, and it was clear, and it was scary.

One of the ways I began to discover my happiness again was through our horsemanship clinics on the weekends. Our clinics would leave me energized, excited, and feeling grateful; all of the things I wanted so badly and expected to feel teaching high school. I discovered my love for teaching again, this time in a whole new way. These realizations were empowering, and yet they did not come without the accompaniment of fear. We will delve deeper into that in chapters to come.

Letting go of a job is one thing, but what if you discover that your bad days are far outweighing your good days due to a toxic romantic relationship? To let go of any relationship can be heart-wrenching, especially one you have been invested in for a long time, emotionally and financially. To top it off, the two of you may have brought little people into this world. Leaving a toxic relationship takes a whole new source of bravery, but is no less imperative to your happiness. Deciding to walk away from romantic relationships of all types is difficult. When we commit to someone, we often set in motion the expectation that our love will last and when the relationship shifts into unhealthy territory the lines of what is right for us become blurred and we begin to accept defeat. Our punishment is to remain in the failed relationship with the intent to "fix it." Not all relationships which fall apart are doomed and cannot be fixed; this is very important to understand.

Being in a relationship with someone is like strapping ourselves into the same car on a roller coaster. There are a few scenarios which may play out for the two people on this ride: One scenario is that they both love the thrill of the ride and they rise and fall together, they laugh, they cry, and they scream in unison while the car takes them places they would rarely choose to go alone. They both experience moments of fear and have faith that they will both come out unscathed on the other side. They both appreciate the slow inclines and embrace each other during the fall. This is ideal, but not entirely relatable for all of us. I know it certainly isn't how my past and present relationship(s) have gone despite my desire for them to do so.

Another scenario may go something like this: Both people hop onto the ride full of excitement for the experience, feeling totally prepared, in tune, and begin hand in hand. At some point, despite the highs, the lows are too much for one to bear. They become desperate to get off, whereas the highs and lows are what the other expected and they barely noticed the struggle of their partner. The one who is unshaken by the unpredictability of the ride thinks their reassuring "You're ok," is all it will take to get the other to calm down and begin to enjoy the experience. When the other hears the words, they become resentful because the words are useless at the time and make them feel unheard and misunderstood, like their experience is not being taken seriously. They let go of their partner's hand, grab the rail in terror, feeling like they are now on a ride alone that they never signed up for. This scenario is not ideal and has the potential to end in a few ways, all depending on how it is handled.

The end result could be to walk away from the ride. They may never understand the perspective of the other, and the end result could be toxic where blame, hate, and a lack of trust reside. Due to this one of them may decide it simply is not for them, and they move onto rides which offer them joy rather than fear.

On the other hand, despite the challenge, with some work both partners get back on the same page, it may take time to heal, however they have the potential to find a point of common understanding through genuine, empathetic, clear communication, and may even find themselves stronger as a result of what they have gone through together.

A final scenario, although there are others, is one where both enter the ride at entirely different points of readiness, expectation, and experience. The ride ends badly from both perspectives. When they get on the ride one may be vibrating with anticipation while the other is shaking in their boots. Nonetheless, they put on a brave face to hide their insecurities and fake being "fine." Maybe in this scenario, they are both faking being fine for different reasons. One is scared the ride will be too long while the other is anxious that it will be too short and not worth their time. Either way, both are entering into it with unspoken fears and expectations which result in them being disconnected from the very start. They both have bad experiences on roller coasters in the past and neither want to admit to the other that they have concerns. They both spend the ride flashing back to past experiences, blaming the other for their current circumstance, and dreaming of something they have no idea how to attain in the future. This experience may result in both recognizing that it was not for them from the start. Not all relationships we decide are not for us end up toxic, and letting go does not have to mean walking away altogether. Maybe they recognize that a romantic relationship is not for them and that opens a door for a great friendship.

Remember that when we let go of something that is no longer right for us, we make room for something new that can bring us joy. This also means that introducing new aspects into our lives sometimes requires letting go of things that no longer serve us well.

In the exercise outlined in this chapter, you will have the opportunity to look at the main triggers of your negative emotions. I want you to remember it is okay to let something go that is not for you. This can be people or circumstances. Know you have the power to change your life but first you have to take an honest look at it.

Exercise:

As you can likely see, clear communication with ourselves is as equally important as clear communication with those around us. I want you to complete an exercise that will not take much time in the beginning, but it may help to shed some light on your happiness. This may require you to invest some time later in discovering more about your well-being.

You will need a calendar which you can access at the end of each day. This may be on your phone or a small one you place by your bed. I personally like to have a calendar I can hold in my hands and write on with a pen. I like to have mine separate from my phone, so I can jot notes and also so it can remain in the same place all the time. It is entirely up to you.

How you want to record the rest is also up to you. I will suggest something I think works very well because it is visual and you can see clearly where you stand:

Place an X on each day you felt was a "bad day." How you determine this is going to be individual, go with your first reaction. Take a minute to tune into how you feel right before you go to bed. What feelings did your day leave you with? Remember, certain situations leave us feeling stronger than others or have the ability to stick with us longer.

Some days you may have nothing in particular that goes terribly wrong, yet you feel down anyway, record that. Other days you may feel like everything you touched went wrong. Despite this, you had a great conversation with your friend or significant other, and they helped you feel good again.

Decipher how you feel at the end of your day and record it. You may leave the days you feel great blank, or place a smiley face, or you could color them with your favorite color, whatever allows you to see how you felt at the end of your day.

It is not a bad idea to jot notes about what you feel "made" your bad days bad. It may help with clarity later on. You may choose to be more specific and break your days into categories. You may record multiple aspects of your days to see which are consistently bringing you happiness and positivity and which are always doing the opposite.

Some daily categories I would suggest (use the ones which suit your life best) are:

- Marriage

- Family Relations

- Friendships

- Work Life

- Recreation

- Free Time

- Finances

It is also helpful to do a quick assessment of all these areas of your life at the start and end of each month to give you a baseline of how you feel within all the important areas of your life every 30 days or so. This is also useful when creating personal growth plans.

Another suggestion I have is to do this for a full year. I know that sounds daunting and maybe completely unlikely, sometimes it feels like we don't even have time to brush our hair each day. This being said, we have time for what we know is absolutely vital to get done. Put this on the vital list. You deserve to take time to acknowledge how you feel. By completing this exercise every day for a year you may notice how the seasonal changes affect your mood and activity level. You may have to take specific actions to maintain a positive mental state at different times throughout the year.

Here is an example of what two different months could look like in the simplified calendar and a more detailed diary (this is an example, not my personal calendar. Let's say it belongs to my imaginary girl, Laine):

Sunday	Monday	Tuesday	Wednesday	Thursday	Friday	Saturday
	1 X Feeling: Tired Ugh, Monday :(	2 X Feeling: Angry Argued with Joe about $	3 :) Feeling: Positive HUMP DAY :) Talked it out	4 X Feeling: Underappreciated at work	5 :) Feeling: Happy! The sun is shining and I ate ice cream	6 :) Feeling: Creative Had time to paint
7 X Feeling: Dread Anxious about work tomorrow	8 :) Feeling: Relieved Didn't see George at work today	9 Feeling: Blessed Had a great family supper	10 :) Feeling: Free Had the day off and painted	11 X Feeling: Upset George is back, he yelled at me as soon as he saw me	12 X Feeling: Overwhelmed I do not have enough time to do what is expected at work	13 X Feeling: Exhausted Took the day to catch up on work
14 X Feeling: Stuck I need to get away	15 X Feeling: Alone Joyce wasn't at work and I needed her	16 :) Feeling: Helpful I helped my friend redecorate their room	17 :) Feeling: Inspired Decided to redecorate our room!	18 X Feeling: Frustrated Joe does not get me :(	19 X Feeling: Annoyed Joe doesn't think I should spend $ on paint.	20 :) Feeling: Cheeky Joe worked so I painted anyway! I LOVE the color!

21	22	23	24	25	26	27
:)	X	X	X	X	:)	:)
Feeling:	Feeling:	Feeling:	Feeling:	Feeling:	Feeling:	Feeling:
Loved	Alone	Worried	Sick	Sick	Re-energized	Good
Made Joe and I supper and he likes the color too.	Joyce wasn't at work again and I had no one to vent to	I don't think I will ever work hard enough for George	Had to go to work anyway!	Still sick and now Joe is too :(	Got lots of rest and the sun is shining	Joe surprised me with fresh flowers

28	29	30	31
X	X	:)	:)
Feeling:	Feeling:	Feeling:	Feeling:
Anxious	Angry	Hopeful	Confident
Why is my boss an ass?	Overall stupid day at work, I can't do it all!	New position just opened up at work, I think I'll apply	Applied for new position at work!

Bad days = 17/31

As you can see the majority of bad days for Laine had resulted from interactions with her boss, George, at work. Had she not taken the time to write out who made her feel the way she did, she may have felt as though she is generally unhappy rather than noticing she is unhappy at her job. Had she not acknowledged her unease at work she may not have applied for the new position and chalked up her unhappiness to be all in her head, the lack of appreciation at work, or an inability to be content.

If we do not take the time to decipher our stresses, we can get caught up in our overall feeling of discontent. This can negatively affect our relationships because we are constantly searching for meaning in relation to our feelings, whether we are conscious of it or not.

It was not until I took the time to mindfully recognize the source of my unhappiness that I realized I wasn't unhappy everywhere and with everything. Once I allowed myself to narrow down my daily triggers of negative emotion, I could separate myself from being an unhappy person, to a person who needed to take a serious look at their work life. It is not that teaching was a terrible job, I went into teaching for a reason. Nevertheless, it is crucial that we recognize when something is no longer a positive service to us. We need to take action to change or walk away so that we can find something else that does serve us well. Much like Laine chose to do.

Here is an example of Laine's calendar after she made some changes:

Sunday	Monday	Tuesday	Wednesday	Thursday	Friday	Saturday
				1 Marriage :) Family :) Friends :) Work Life :I Leisure :)	2 :) Feeling: Great George was gone today and I helped Ash design her nursery	3 :) Feeling: Happy Joe and I had a great day trip to the city
4 :) Feeling: Relaxed Had lunch with my girls	5 :) Feeling: Awesome! GOT AN INTERVIEW	6 X Feeling: Doubtful What if I don't get it? What if I am not good enough?	7 X Feeling: Mad but determined I BETTER get this new job!	8 :) Feeling: Amazing! GOT THE JOB!	9 :) Feeling: Grateful So happy I have a new opportunity	10 :) Feeling: Loved Celebrated with friends and family at home
11 X Feeling: Frustrated Everything I touched today went wrong	12 :) Feeling: Better Cleaned out my office today and cleaned the house	13 X Feeling: Overwhelmed and tired Need to get this move done!	14 :) Feeling: Positive Met my new boss and she seems like my kind of person	15 :) Feeling: Relieved Love my new workspace and coworkers	16 :) Feeling: Happy Joe and I went on a date after work <3	17 X Feeling: Sad Lost a family member today :(

18	19	20	21	22	23	24
X	X	X	:)	:)	:)	X
Feeling: Lost/Guilty	Feeling: Anxious/sad	Feeling: Like life is not fair :(	Feeling: More myself	Feeling: Lighter	Feeling: Good	Feeling: Nostalgic
I wish I had called Claire last week :(	Have to speak at the funeral tomorrow		Joe and I took the day off together and watched movies all day	Back to work and everyone was so kind	Getting into the swing of things at work and painted tonight	Can't believe she has been gone a week. I miss her :(

25	26	27	28	29	30	31
:)	:)	:)	:)	:)	:)	:)
Feeling: Supported	Feeling: Renewed	Feeling: Awesome!	Feeling: Productive	Feeling: Creative	Feeling: Balanced	Feeling: Blessed
Received a couple very kind messages today and went to Ash's baby shower	Started a new book and someone asked me to redecorate their daughter's room- they want to pay me?!	Work was great and started my new project. It felt like I could feel Claire with me today.	Showed Ryan my concept for his daughter's room and he loved it.	Opened a social media account for my interior designs.	Got up early for a walk, had a good day at work and had a new message asking how much I charge for interior make-overs!	Life is good, despite the rain :)

Bad days = 9/31

Laine chose to take action. Despite the very emotional and challenging circumstance of losing someone important to her, she was still able to maintain a better bad-to-good day ratio than the month before. It is clear that her new positive energy allowed her the space to expand on the things which she enjoyed most and she was inspired to publicize her love for creative design.

It is worth noting that despite making a very positive change some days were still difficult and stressful. We must not expect our decisions, even the good ones, or may I even state especially the good ones, to be stress-free. When we listen to our hearts and push ourselves past our edges, then we will always be trying new and exciting things which make our hearts pound and our heads spin. With a mindful approach, these feelings will help us gauge when we are growing and will make us feel alive.

Just as an owner may come to the conclusion their horse is not for them, a partner discovers their relationship is past the point of saving, or an employee recognizes their mental health is worth more than the security their job has to offer, we need to know when to quit.

Quitting holds such a negative connotation in our society. When we begin to realize something is unhealthy for us, our ego reminds us that "no one likes a quitter," "quitters never win," and so on. We convince ourselves that quitting is not what is best simply by using the word quit. Let's remove that word from the circumstance of leaving a situation that is not best suited to us. It is not quitting, in the negative sense of the word, when we are moving forward.

Do not allow the thoughts of others or, often more damaging, your own thoughts shaped and formed by our negative comparisons to others, to convince you to stay in a situation that is not right for you. It is important to note: Just because something was right for you yesterday, last year, or ten years ago, does not mean it is still right for you today. You have the right to change.

CHAPTER SIX

The Importance of Energy

*"The higher your energy level, the more efficient your body.
The more efficient your body, the better you feel and the more
you will use your talent to produce outstanding results."*

Tony Robbins

We discuss energy with people and their horses at every one of
our horsemanship clinics. Horses can read our energy from the
moment they see us. Establishing a great relationship with a horse
often starts when we become aware and responsible for our own
energy, plus the ability to recognize the energy of our horse and
how to use ours to influence it.

As much as our energy influences horses, those around us are equally affected. Until I began noticing a drastic decline in my own energy, I had not put much thought into the importance it played in my health and well-being.

For this chapter, I will talk about who we communicate with, more so than how we interact with them. When we take the time to think about the people we communicate with most, we will see another form of conscious communication. This chapter will help us become aware of and responsible for the energy we present to others which comes out in our movement, our voice, our actions, and our words, and how it affects those around us and vice versa.

A step toward mindful communication is being responsible for how we affect others with our energy and also how others affect us. I had not thought about the energy I bring into a room, how my energy affects others, or what made the changes in my own energy until I felt a drastic change in how I was feeling and interacting.

Growing up I was always a pretty upbeat person. Days that I felt like I had less energy than normal, I chalked up to a lack of sleep or sickness coming on. I did not attribute it to the influence of my thoughts, other people, or my environment. It wasn't until I delved further into my personal development journey that I began to investigate energy a little further.

Until this point, I had put no time into understanding the importance of energy on a larger scale and how universal energy influenced the direction of my life. I knew energy existed around me. I had power in my home. I used a cell phone. I had a toddler who would go from wildly happy to melting on the floor mad in a matter of seconds. There were people who I loved being around, and there were people who made me feel less myself when I was with them. Energy is something we tend to think little of on a personal level because it is not tangible, but we know it is there.

It was not until I began investing my time into learning how to change my life that I began to learn that my energy renewal came from within, that others' energy could greatly affect my own, and that my energy is not only connected to other peoples' but to the entire universe.

To be honest, I became so interested that my new knowledge slightly consumed me. I was also somewhat annoyed that I had not known about all this life-changing information far sooner. As I continued to learn, I then discovered why I had not learned about what is known as the law of attraction sooner. I would not have been ready. The right people did not surround me. I was not in a place that I was open to learning or felt the need to learn about it. The universe gives us what we need precisely when we need it. It is up to us to recognize and act on the opportunities presented. And it was finally my time to act.

I will give you a brief explanation of the law of attraction. If you already know of it, it will serve as a reminder of what you are working with, if this is your first time hearing of it, this may be your time, as it was mine to begin to work with it consciously. If you read this and you think it is bogus, that is okay. You may not be ready for this information at this time. Read it and put it into the back of your mind, it may serve you when you are in a place that is more aligned with the information you are receiving here.

Law of Attraction

I first heard of the law of attraction when I was in high school, and my grandmother bought me the book *The Secret*, written by Rhonda Byrne. I don't think I opened a page. In my mid-twenties I was in a place in my life where I was searching for what was next. I was happy with my life overall, though I was struggling with a difficult relationship with an important family member and I had a hard time processing that I needed to let go. I needed someone to tell me how to handle the situation with an unbiased opinion.

A close friend of mine and I decided to do what every answer searching young adult does—maybe not all, but we thought it was a great idea—we called a psychic. This was not necessarily the best tactic in the eyes of some. However, I had not learned yet to trust my intuition, so I looked for answers in other ways, and I thoroughly enjoyed this method. It was during a reading that I was told to watch the movie *The Shift* by Dr. Wayne Dyer. I had not heard of the film nor Wayne Dyer and quickly jotted down the names on my paper. At the time, I did not see how her suggestion to watch this film and my reading were connected.

I see now this was the first time I was open enough to receive the information, but I still wasn't quite ready for it entirely. I looked up the movie and watched half of it, and while I was watching it, I was only half interested in what I was watching. A few years later someone bought me the book *The Secret* for the second time. I did not finish the book at that time either. I then began watching the movie *The Secret,* and you guessed it, I didn't finish it. I was intrigued by the concepts but was not open to understanding them in relation to my life and my problems. I may have been struggling with a bit of accountability.

It was not until I turned 30 that I began to make the shift into understanding and then consciously and actively using the law to my advantage. It is important to recognize that the law was always affecting my life, I was, however, not aware of how my thoughts were creating my reality, so I was not deliberately creating my life. I was reacting to it.

By definition: *The law of attraction can best be explained as universal energy which obeys the science of physics based on these three principles: 1) everything is energy; 2) energy follows thought; 3) what you focus on you get more of. We are like cosmic magnets. Our thoughts and feelings send out a vibration, and universal energy matches our vibration by giving us more of the same, resonant energy. The human energy system includes the upward and downward flow of universal energy into the human body and the seven major chakras . . . which attach to the spinal column. These and other parts of our energy system are very dynamic and change quickly based on what we think and feel. If our thoughts are not positive, our energy system reacts by pulling in negative energy and can become blocked. Old behavior patterns repeat themselves, preventing us from moving towards our greatest intentions. When our energy system is clear, however, we are able to project positive energy, one of the key elements required to fulfill the law of attraction.*[25]

When I opened fully to knowing the law of attraction, I was going through the process of reading, asking questions, and connecting—the most valuable part of my process—when I noticed a yo-yo effect happening within me from Monday to Friday. As I previously mentioned, I had created a space in my home that I would go to early in the morning, before the rest of the house rose for the day, and I would drink my tea, focus on my intentions for the day, express my gratitude, write, and work on a coaching course I had signed up for. It was incredible to feel the change in my energy. I had sparked a light and reconnected with myself. I was wearing my new approach to life like a bright white aura that everyone could see. However, this aura would be gone by the end of my day. I would physically feel the energy I started my day with drain away as I marked assignments that did not show effort, as I refocused student after student away from their phone and back to their work, as I talked to other teachers who had visibly lost their spark, as I planned lessons I knew I was putting more time into then would be appreciated, and as I fielded already answered question after already answered question.

My energy was fluctuating from high frequency to low frequency so much throughout the day that I began to feel like I was losing balance again. I would wake up and feel inspired then leave my work day feeling deflated. I knew the answer was in my new-found practices of self-care. I also knew that to maintain a feeling of purpose and joy I had to commit to making a change in my life.

As I understood the importance to create change to shift my energy entirely, I set a new goal to maintain as high vibration as possible. I knew teaching was stopping me from doing so. This realization was one of many that ensured I was making the right choice by leaving my job. I discovered that the environment and demands it placed on me as an individual did not align with my needs. Some people maintain a high vibration *because* of their teaching job; it is all based on the individual, and we all function differently in different environments.

I discovered I needed to have the ability to be more selective of the type of energetic beings I was dedicating my days to. As a teacher I had every kind of person enter my room, and they influenced both the room and myself. Negative energy is stronger than positive energy, and I could feel it fill my classroom as certain groups of unmotivated, seemingly unhappy students entered. I felt their influence on me and did not fully understand why.

One day I stumbled upon a website called *Accidental Creative*, where they had shared a guest essay by Sarah Kathleen Peck.[26] I connected with her words immediately. She very clearly described the types of energies I was interacting with on a regular basis. It helped me to understand why I dreaded some classes entering my room even though they were not behaviorally difficult. I had a sinking feeling as they approached my class and knew it would be a challenge to teach them.

In her essay, Peck broke down the vibrational levels people operated on and the influence they have on those around them. It made me understand why I felt the need to create a life where I was free from an environment where I had so many people in my space at once with no reprieve. I could identify every student based on their energy after reading her article. I discovered that in my classroom, no matter how much positive energy I emitted, I was being filled with overpowering negative energy on a regular basis.

Peck broke people down as energetic beings into the following profiles:

Energy Profiles by Sarah Peck[27]

The Positives	The Middle Balance (Balancers & Grounders)	Negatives
Buzzers • These are my excited electrons. People who are so thrilled to be around other people and in the world, talking with them is like getting a burst of inspiration. When I wake up in the morning, a phone call with them is better than coffee. They are my muses, my inspirations, my creatives. Like coffee, however, I can't drink it nonstop each day – so they are better in quantifiable bursts	**Quiet Stabilizers** • People who are refreshing, rejuvenating, and inspiring without being showy or ostentatious. Someone you can sit quietly in a park with, without talking very much, and leave happier. These people don't toot their own horn, and likely don't know how cool they are. Yet being around them is satiating, relaxing, restorative.	**The Repetitives & Non-Changers** • People who are stuck in a problem that you've listened to for years. Their complaints are the same, over and over again, and they don't bring anything new to the table. Each time, it feels like you're stuck in déjà-vu, because you're still talking about how to deal with their terrible relationships, bad work situation, or general malaise. To deal with these types, tell them, politely and firmly, that you don't want to talk about their _____ problem anymore. "I appreciate all the struggles you are having with your job situation, but I'd like to not talk about that anymore. I know you are working hard on it. Let's focus and talk about new things when we meet."

Happys	Feedbacks	The Fakes
• Generally positive, seem to be happy almost all the time. People you would skip with, laugh with, enjoy being with. I have lots of these in my life. They aren't as physically excited as the Buzzers, but they are generally happy and have a positive attitude about most things.	• People who tell you what you need to hear, not necessarily what you want to hear. These people can be mistakenly labeled as negatives, but they still have your best interests in heart and are actually looking out for you in the long run. Keep them around, but note the times when you aren't up for receiving feedback and need encouragement instead – and seek them out when you need smart advice.	• There are people who masquerade as positives – the words they use are cheery, they tell you what they think you want to hear; they quote inspirational things and bits. But the substance is not there. And, more importantly, you are not rejuvenated by the words or the ideas in the way you are around Quiet Wonders or Listeners or Buzzers. Some people are obviously fake; others not so obviously. At the end of the day, what's most important is how you respond when you're around them.
Wonder Listeners	**The Strugglers & Changers**	**Negative Influences**
• People who can hear what you are saying without you saying it; who seem to listen to you with both their bodies and their ears, and who exude a positive radiance without necessarily saying or doing anything, are your Wonder Listeners. After hanging out with one of these, I leave feeling happy, excited, and inspired.	• There are people who are struggling, working toward change, and are sometimes frustrated or caught in-betweens. They are on their way toward becoming the person they want to be, and conversations with them are raw, open, inspiring, hard, and generally variable. These are my strongest friends, the people who open my eyes and listen to my shared experiences as well. We learn well together. To note, however, sometimes I don't have enough energy to devote to these conversations, and it's best to say No and save the date for another, more energetic time.	• There are people who are wonderful, interesting, bright, and creative. And yet, for some reason, I am negatively influenced when I am around them. It's not that they themselves are bad people – it's that I make bad choices when I'm around them. For some reason or another, hanging out with them is not conducive to my success. These are the trickiest people to identify, because there's nothing about them that's bad or easy to rationalize avoiding. It's how they influence you that tells you about whether or not it's a good person to have in your life.

Coaches & Mentors		Toxic
• These are people who seem to have endless stores of hope and inspiration designed just for you. People who are genuinely interested in what you have to offer and how you are doing. The coaches and mentors are usually a check-in, once a week or once a month, and they offer their advice and wisdom to you in their interactions.		• These are the people who make you feel like shutting down when you're around them. The people that drain you, that zap your energy, that are filled with negativity and cutting remarks. Most of us quickly eliminate these people from our lives after just a few interactions. They are easy to spot and identify. If you still have them around, ask yourself why? What do you benefit from being with a toxic person?

Note: The "I" within this chart is that of the original author Sarah Peck and this was used with her permission. My personal experience is detailed below.

When I assessed my experience as a teacher and the types of people I was interacting with daily I came to some conclusions: First, that I believe people can be a combination of these energies and also that I have only had the privilege of teaching a few people who I would consider "Buzzers." However, Peck's explanation showed why I loved having them leave my classroom just as much as I loved seeing them enter. In my experience teachers who can be described as "Buzzers" are the ones who stay in the profession with the most enthusiasm. They seem to overpower the other energies in the room and are easily recharged to continue teaching in a dynamic way. This is the type of teacher I strived to be, and I discovered relatively quickly I was not that person naturally, so I would never be able to sustain it throughout my teaching days.

In my life outside of the classroom, I have quite a few "Happys," although I have met fewer and fewer of these types of people at the high school level throughout my years of teaching. The teachers who I have encountered and would describe as "Happys" are the ones I have always befriended and relied on for emotional support.

I have also only encountered a few "Wonder Listeners" in my classroom. This may be because of the nature of the school. It does not allow for this type of person to have as strong of an influence as if they were in a more one-on-one setting. I also had not actively looked for this type of person in my classroom because I did not rely on my students for personal support. I have encountered a few of these as colleagues, not surprisingly, they have often been the guidance counselors.

When I read of the "Coaches and Mentors" I discovered that I had seen a number of students who are this to other students, but again due to the nature of my position in the classroom I did not look to them for this relationship. They did tend to be much less energetically draining and made me feel at ease when they entered my room. I have also met a few colleagues who fit into this category. Most often they were the administrators who hired me despite my lack of experience early on; they did so based merely on their belief that I was capable of the job.

I have seen "Quiet Stabilizers" struggle in high school as students. They are not as loud and forward as some. They often got overlooked, but I had seen them become more appreciated by their peers as they get closer to graduation when they began to appreciate their energy and what they had to offer. Personally, I am drawn to these people in and out of work. I would have loved to work more with those who fell into this category. Unfortunately, the structure of teaching does not lend itself to a lot of collaborative time. I do believe this may be part of why I found the teaching environment challenging at times. As I have expanded my personal connections, I have paid close attention to when I meet these people, and I take special note of my attraction to them and their importance in my life.

When I think of "Feedbacks," I have one particular student that comes to mind. She was harsh, yet so soft. I admired her dedication to her group of friends. Sadly, her need to help them often took from her own productivity, and she would get lost in others' problems. I have met numerous teachers who share this energy. After all, we are trained to give feedback. I personally can relate here as well. I often find myself giving rational advice and feedback to friends. I have had to become aware of when they are ready for this and when it is best left unsaid. Recognizing myself as a "Feedback" has also allowed me to soften in my approach to others. I am now able to recognize when I have come back at someone with feedback that is too quick, too abrupt, or too much. I have to work on this daily.

I also identify with the "Strugglers and Changers" and outside of teaching, these people are my closest friends. These are the people who open my eyes and listen to my shared experiences. On the other hand, they have been my most common and challenging type of student. As adults, we learn well together, yet sometimes I don't have enough energy to give to our conversations and must save them for a more energetic time. Unfortunately, this is not possible for a teacher. I was there to help when they needed it, whether I had the energy for them or not. I often felt like I connected with these students though never enough to make a difference in their lives. I have struggled greatly with this throughout the years.

It was "Negatives" who influenced me the most. So, I have come to understand how important it is for me to be mindful of my thoughts and my communication. I have, since leaving teaching, learned how to ground myself, protect my personal energy and release the energy that is not mine. These tools would have been incredibly useful prior to leaving.

The "Repetitives and Non-Changers" were the most draining for me, in and out of work. Here is a great example of two concepts we have discussed so far: Being soft and saying "this is not for me." It can feel unsupportive to shut someone down from expressing their complaints, however, if we are looking to take control of our own happiness, this is an absolute must. We have to recognize when someone is a "Non-Changer" and that their negative energy is depleting our positive energy because their energy overpowers ours. It is imperative that we take responsibility for our own energy while interacting with these people and hope that our shift of the conversation to something more positive will refocus them. As a teacher, it was very challenging to take control of these conversations as I should because it was often difficult for students to understand their effect on others. As a teacher, I risked coming off as uncaring, dismissive, or mean.

When I met "Fakes" I tended to say to myself or sometimes out loud to a friend, "I know I should like this person, and they have done nothing wrong, but there is just something about them." That feeling of something being off was a warning that they were not genuine. I have encountered many of these students. Mostly toward the end of the semester when they needed something from me for them to pass my course. Their positive tone and smiles appeared more manipulative than they did inviting. I had a tough time with these people outside of work because until recently I had a tough time trusting my intuition. It has taken some hurtful situations to learn the lesson to trust my heart when I sense something is off with someone I meet.

"Negatives" are also tough because it takes some pretty strong self-awareness to see when someone has a poor influence over us, even if they are not entirely bad for us. If we find we are influenced by someone we spend time with in ways that slow our growth, make us question ourselves, or our values, they are not necessarily negative; they are a negative influence. It is important that we also realize these people may be a lot of fun, but if they are misaligning us with our success, we have to let them go.

Others who are vital to let go of are the "Toxic" people in our lives. It is important to distance ourselves as much as possible from toxic people. It is also important to note that: "*When a toxic person can no longer control you, they will try to control how others see you. The misinformation will feel unfair, stay above it, trusting that other people will eventually see the truth, just like you did.*"[28] When we discover someone is toxic for us, remember they may not be toxic for everyone. It can be challenging to let them go but crucial for us to be happy. We must mindfully interact with them when we have to and work to maintain our own power in our personal lives. I have found that these sort of people tend to come with a history and when we need, for our well-being, to step away. Time is our ally. We do not need to feel like we have to just cut these people out in one day. It may be necessary in extreme cases certainly, but not in all. We may contribute less to their conversations, we may call or message less often, and we may begin to put our positive energy into healthier people for us. We are in control. I have spoken with women who expressed the difficulty in letting go of a toxic family member. I have also witnessed the shift in them when they have taken action.

When I was a teacher, I felt less and less control over the energy of my classroom. In the past, I felt that if I greeted my students with positive energy at the door that it would lift the energy in the room and create a positive environment. I question whether I felt that I had more influence in the past because of the age group I was dealing with. I began teaching junior high school, where I seemed to have more of an emotional impact on them. This seemed to also change with the greater presence of cell phones. In my early years of teaching my students would enter my room asking about assignments or class work, or even how I was doing. This became less as my students became older and more engrossed in their social lives. I have seen students unable to disconnect from their lives outside of the classroom to allow them to connect to their education.

Through some self-reflection, I discovered that I am not naturally the type of person who can rise above continuous negative energy. I find it very difficult to maintain my own sense of self when I am not able to control my social environment. As I became more aligned with who I truly am and how I shape my life I began to notice shifts in how others perceived me.

After some major mental shifts as a result of working with my personal life coach, I had a grade nine student approach me at my desk. It was before the bell, and she was getting her poetry portfolio out of the cupboard by my desk. Once she had her materials and said good morning, I noticed her lingering a little longer as if she wanted to speak to me. I made eye contact with her, and she told me how much she enjoyed coming to my class because it is so "peaceful." I asked her why she felt this way and she said, "Because of you." We carried on the conversation, and I expressed my gratitude and appreciation for her kind words. It was not until later that evening when I was crawling into bed that the word she used made its impact. *Peaceful.*

We feel peaceful when we are free from disturbance. We feel peaceful when we are safe. We feel peaceful when we are calm. If anyone were to ask me to describe any of my classes in one word, peaceful would never enter my mind. This beautiful interaction reminded me of valuable lessons: I affect others as much as they affect me and changing my mindset could change my reality.

Before the conversation mentioned above with my grade nine student, it had been a long time since I could reflect on the positive in my classroom. I was so caught up in how my whole day felt, such a flux of mood and emotion for so long; I could not see the shift that happened once I began to take personal responsibility for my thoughts and communication.

Taking Control

If you think about the people who are around you the most, you may notice that some have a calming effect on you, whereas others will make you feel anxious by entering the room. It is important for us to understand why we feel this way when we interact with specific people because it will allow us the opportunity to interact with them appropriately.

If we do not take the time to understand how a specific person's energy affects us, we are simply affected. We can find ourselves searching for meaning in the wrong places while we are with them. Keep in mind that our minds are meaning makers. If we have a feeling, we will try to sort out why. By understanding how we are influenced by others' energy, we attain the ability to tell ourselves exactly why we are feeling the way we are and by doing so we have the potential to avoid conflict or misunderstandings.

My husband naturally possesses a much higher energy than me. This is most apparent in the morning. He wakes up every day as if he has never had a bad day. He reminds me each day to appreciate the people who are closest to us by simply wanting to speak to me when he opens his eyes. We balance each other out.

The only time that our energies do not work well together is during times when he or I am feeling overwhelmed. When he feels overwhelmed, I can tell as soon as he enters the house. I can tell by how his feet hit the stairs, how his voice sounds when he first speaks, or better yet, doesn't speak at all, and most significantly the urgency in which he does anything and everything in that moment. In the early years of our relationship, I found when he entered the house in this way I immediately felt tense.

Before becoming more mindful in my communication and furthering my understanding of how others affect me, this was a sure sign an argument would start. Him being overwhelmed made me overwhelmed, and it was difficult for me to figure out why I felt so defensive out of the blue. I could feel myself begin to search for meaning for his mood, and for the shift in mine. In my head, I would tell myself to run and do things that made it look like there was less to do. I would come up with reasons I did not get specific things done. I would be on the defense no matter what he said because I felt like I had done something to make him feel the way he did. Wow. That would all happen before I asked him what was wrong or before he had the chance to tell me himself.

Today if he came home in this state I would have to talk myself through my communication with him. I spent so long taking responsibility for other peoples' energy that I still require some pretty serious self-talk to maintain my own positive energy, and by doing so it allows for much easier conversations during difficult times, and I am not always successful. I still become defensive and reactive at times because often I still find myself searching for personal responsibility for the energy other people bring to me. I have to remind myself that we are all a work in progress. Sometimes I catch myself sinking into thoughts like: *What did I do? I must have done something wrong,* or the most damaging for our communication and relationships, *I don't know what their problem is!*? When I catch myself thinking this way now, I try to reassess the situation and look at it from a new perspective. I try to detach myself from it and redirect my thoughts to ways I can help them or help myself. If I think I may be able to help them, I will ask, "Are you okay?" or "Is there something I can do to make the situation better?" or "Can I help?" If I ask Mike this, it is normally answered with a quick, "Yes!" and a large list. I feel good when I can ease his mind, and it is much more productive than walking by on my way to the bathroom to avoid him and grumbling a, "What's your problem?"

If it is a person other than my spouse, I take their answer for what it is, and I try to move on. If they do not need me, based on their responses to my questions, then I have done my part, and I need to be responsible for my own energy and not dwell on what my ego may try to tell me about what they might be mad about.

When I am overwhelmed, I am usually hyper-sensitive to my husband's energy. It does not take much for him to send me into tears, certainly not intentional on his part. My reaction to him during my times of overwhelm is not his responsibility. They are mine, and I am coming to terms with this. Sometimes the reaction, however, isn't such a bad thing. Sometimes I have been holding in too much emotion and really needed to let it out. When this happens, I cry, and when I need it to happen it doesn't take much; a weird look or a comment my ego can bend in a way to make it offensive, even when it was not intended to be. He has learned to soften with me in these times, and his reaction is what brings me back to a grateful state which usually helps shift me somewhat out of my overwhelm and into a more productive emotional state.

Might Mode: Equally as Dangerous as Flight Mode

Let's talk about "maybes" for a moment. They are not healthy for us. "Maybe" should be erased from our vocabulary because it creates uncertainty, non-commitment, and inaccuracy.

Here are three of the most destructive ways we use the word maybe, both with ourselves and others: "Maybe they are mad at me," "Maybe I'll do that later," and in response to someone else asking us for something, "Maybe." Each statement sets us up for failure and creates gray communication within our own mind and the minds of other's.

We will start with the first statement: "Maybe they are mad at me." As you can probably guess, this can be modified to fit anyone we are talking to ourselves about. It is damaging when it is being used in reference to someone who is close to us, a friend, lover, or family member. Normally, we allow ourselves to think this when something has happened that we don't understand and we feel the need to make sense of it. For example, we drive by, and they seem to look at us, yet don't wave or they text back a one-word answer with a period. You know what I'm talking about. You have a text conversation with someone, and they end it with an, "Ok." And our minds go wild! We immediately begin to search for meaning in what we interpret as a short response. We read it in a tone that we think suits the grammar and we panic. When we get a response that does not seem to suit the tone of the conversation we often go into "might mode", simply searching for meaning. Horses have a similar response system which we call "flight mode." They go into self-preservation mode and begin to search for answers in a less constructive way than we desire, much like ourselves when we go into "might mode."

When we are working with horses, we work to bring them out of flight mode by showing them how to use the thinking side of their brain. This shows us that we need to train ourselves to react less and think more. Not just any thinking, but constructive thinking. One of the unhealthiest habits we create is the habit of overreaction. When we overreact we create unnecessary drama, negative emotional responses, and undue stress for ourselves and others. We must remember that we are also sending out the vibration of what we will get more of—overreaction. We need to think responsibly.

When we begin to wonder what might be wrong in situations, we send ourselves into a state of worry. Often, we later discover that we worried for nothing. When we catch ourselves searching for meaning through the use of "maybe" and "might" we need to recognize that it is not active problem solving, it is simply creating negative feelings in us which influence our mood and our day.

When something occurs that sends us into this state, we should take action if possible. We should call the friend we are concerned we offended or look for a solution to find a true answer to settle our worry as soon as possible. If we cannot or will not do something to find an answer to our "mights" we should use Mel Robbins's *The 5 Second Rule*, which will be discussed in the next chapter, to help change our thoughts to something more serving and productive.

The second destructive "maybe" I mentioned was, "Maybe I'll do it later." This statement immediately puts us into non-action mode. We stall ourselves from taking responsibility, doing what is needed, and creating a healthy balance. "Maybe I'll do it later," almost always sets me up to be overwhelmed down the road. I end up with everything piling up on my plate all at once, and it results in unneeded stress. Had I committed to taking action when I first thought of something needing to be done, I would feel organized and on the ball rather than pressed for time and out of sorts.

I think the most damaging way that "Maybe I'll do it later" is used is in regard to things we would *love* to do but allow excuses of any sort to stop us from doing. For example, "You are an incredible artist, you should create a piece to auction off!" You leave the conversation feeling inspired and rather than taking immediate inspired action, you put it off and risk never taking action at all.

Inspired action is the cure to eliminating "Maybe I'll do it later." It does not mean we need to drop everything every time we get an idea, but it does suggest that we take an initial step to set a plan into motion. Some small actions that kick things into gear are giving your card or number to someone, asking someone to call you with more information, adding someone on social media, sending a quick note to someone who may be able to help you, setting a reminder in your phone to remind yourself of how you are feeling at the moment, calling a friend and telling them about your idea, or taking a photo to add it to your vision board. Any little thing that lights a spark of connection to prevent the idea from only ever being an idea and never coming to fruition.

When we use "maybe" as a response to being asked to do something by someone else it is the epitome of non-commitment and shows a lack of care, want, or priority. When we say "maybe" to a request from a friend we leave the reason for our response up for interpretation, and we run the risk of our gray communication sending a message we did not intend.

When we say "maybe" rather than "no" because, honestly, who likes to say no, we set loose boundaries. Our answer is left up to interpretation, our "maybe" could say, "I don't want to, but push me a little harder and you will successfully guilt me into a yes." Or it could say, "What you need me for is less important than other things I *might* have the opportunity to do, if nothing better comes up, then yes." This interpretation typically hurts feelings where hurt feelings were never intended and could have been prevented by a definite no with an honest reason why.

Saying no is difficult at times for some of us because we don't want to disappoint others, but why leave the answer up to them as a result of our gray communication? When we say "maybe" we are putting off the inevitable response we already know in our minds, and for some reason or another, want to put off for a better time. But is there ever really a better time? Say no when you need to say no to prevent others from walking all over you or unintentionally sending negative messages to friends and family.

When we say "maybe" rather than "yes," we quiet the desires in our heart, we rid ourselves of opportunity, and we shut doors. A "maybe" is enough for someone to believe we are uninterested when, on the inside, we were jumping up and down. Do not play it cool with a "maybe," do not feign disinterest for any reason with a "maybe."

We need to allow ourselves to say "YES" when we want to. Perhaps we want to say yes but have other obligations and so our yes comes out as a maybe. Eliminate the "maybe." Be honest with yourself and the person you are talking to. Tell them you really would love to, but you have something you are scheduled to do. Be sure they know to ask you again if the opportunity arises. Be honest, and you will save others from coming up with their own reasons for your response, as I discussed in the previous paragraph. Allow yourself to say yes to more things in life. Yes is an empowering word. When you begin saying yes when you normally would hold back and say no, you will surprise yourself with how freeing it is.

I was asked recently, "Do you want to go to a retreat in Costa Rica?" My heart screamed YES, and I felt my brain kick in with all the reasons to reduce it to a maybe. *You can't say yes, just say maybe, you don't know if you can afford it, it's not for a long time, you can let them know later, what if no one can go with you, you can't do that trip alone, definitely say MAYBE, a YES is far too risky.* Thanks, but no thanks brain.

I decided not to allow fear to dictate my answer for once. I shut down all of the want to say maybe, and I said YES. Without any answers, I said yes. After I said yes, I went back to all the fears my brain told me and I began solving them. I told myself I could save what I need in a year to make the trip feasible. I posted on social media and found a friend to join me on the adventure. The idea that it was a long time away and that I had time to let them know was one of my biggest pushes to say yes.

How often do we use time as a buffer for our fears and then allow ourselves to let the excitement fade and eventually convince ourselves it wasn't going to be that great anyway? I was not allowing that to happen this time.

We hide behind "maybe" for so many reasons. Bring your awareness to why you feel the need to say maybe in the future. Translate it to your real answer and feel yourself breathe a sigh of relief. Feel your energy shift with the assuredness of the words "yes" and "no." Relieve yourself of the low energy "maybe" brings into your life.

Exercise:

If you discover throughout this exercise that you are not bringing the type of energy to others that you know you can, then mindfully and gradually change. Give yourself permission to change. We have the ability to grow, and mindful communication is a small step in the right direction. Be honest with yourself. Know that what we bring to others energetically is a direct result of our mindset and that can change with consistent mindset work. Some of it comes from our natural personality which will be challenging to change and not always necessary.

When I began teaching I pictured myself as a "Buzzer" and admired others who were. I saw their impact on students and what their energy brought to the learning environment. Despite my great desire to offer that energy to my students it was simply too foreign to my personality to be able to achieve on a consistent basis, or at all. I do have a tendency to fall into a more negative energy pattern at times. It takes some pretty deep self-awareness or a conversation with someone I trust and respect to help me see the cause and the solution. The more in tune we are with our own energy, the more in tune we will be with others, and what we want, or don't want to subject ourselves to.

Remember our thoughts create our feelings. When we connect this back to clear and conscious communication, we can see it all starts within ourselves. We must communicate clearly with ourselves to communicate effectively with others. When we understand the power we possess over our own reality we see the importance of becoming more deliberate in our thoughts, our words, and our actions, and how this positively affects our relationships.

Complete this exercise when you have time alone to think and feel. Have your journal and an open mind with you. Below you will see a copy of the chart from earlier in the chapter. There are spaces for you to write if you feel so inclined, or you can copy your answers into your journal.

First, think about how you feel. Do you feel high energy, happy, low energy, or stuck? How you feel will determine how you affect others, how you live into your power, and your potential.

Which energy category do you fall in?

Below you will find space to look at the people you surround yourself with. In the spaces below jot the names of all the people who apply:

1. The people you interact with daily in person:
2. The people you interact with daily through text, phone, facetime, messaging:

3. The people you wish you could interact with daily in person:
4. The people you wish you didn't have to interact with daily in person:
5. The people you wish you didn't have to interact with daily through text, phone, facetime, messaging:

Take the names of the people you have listed above in the exercise and place them accordingly into the chart:

The Positives	The Middles (Balancers & Grounders)	Negatives
Buzzers • Like excited electrons, they are thrilled to be around others and we may even feel a burst of inspiration just speaking with them. • Act like a boost to our energy but are best in doses as they are difficult to interact with for long periods of time.	**Quiet Stabilizers** • Feel refreshing and inspiring without being showy. • Someone we could sit quietly with without speaking much and leave happier and content. • Not boastful and likely don't know how great they really are.	**The Repetitives & Non-Changers** • Stuck in a problem that seems to never end. • Complaints seldom change and they don't try to actively solve them. • Have a difficult time seeing how they are a part of a problem rather than part of a solution.

Happys	Feedbacks	The Fakes
• Generally positive. • Aren't as physically excited as the buzzers, however they are mostly happy and have a positive attitude about things. _____ _____ _____ _____ _____	• Tell us what we need to hear just not necessarily what we want to hear. • Approach can at times result in them being labeled as negative but they have our best interests at heart. _____ _____ _____ _____ _____ _____ _____	• Hide behind the mask of being positive. • When we spend time with these people we are not inspired or energized by their ideas and words despite their positive nature, the substance is not there. _____ _____ _____
Wonder Listeners	**Strugglers & Changers**	**Negative Influences**
• Seem to hear what you are saying even without you saying it. • Seem to listen to you with their whole selves and emit a positivity without even speaking. • After we spend time with one of these individuals we are likely to leave feeling happy, excited, or inspired. _____ _____ _____ _____ _____ _____ _____ _____	• Working toward change and are at times conflicted because they are on the road to becoming the person they want to be. • Conversations with these people are often raw, open, inspiring, and sometimes hard. _____ _____ _____ _____ _____ _____ _____ _____ _____ _____ _____ _____	• May be many positive things like fun, intriguing, smart, and creative. Interestingly, we are negatively influenced by them. • Person may not be bad however when we are around them we make bad choices and our time together is not conducive to our success. • Difficult to identify because there is nothing that speaks badly about them, it is just how they influence you as a person. _____ _____ _____ _____

Coaches & Mentors	Notes:	Toxic
• Seem to offer hope and inspiration designed specifically for us.	_____ _____ _____	• A lot easier to identify than the negative influences.
• Genuinely interested in what we have to offer and how we are doing.	_____ _____ _____	• Suck the energy from us and fill us with negativity.
• Offer advice and wisdom to us in their interactions.	_____ _____	_____
_____ _____ _____ _____ _____ _____ _____	_____ _____ _____ _____ _____ _____	_____ _____ _____ _____ _____ _____

Note: Peck's categories are paraphrased/shortened in this chart for the purpose of this exercise.

Take a look at where the people you interact with the most fall. Assess how they serve or take away from you energetically.

CHAPTER SEVEN

Fear: The Quintessential Dream Crusher

"Being brave isn't the absence of fear.
Being brave is having that fear,
but finding a way through it."

Bear Grylls

Fear can and will creep in and control our lives if we allow it. If we listen to fear, it will stifle us and make us see the world from a pessimistic view rather than a positive one. I see fear limit relationships with horses over and over again.

One way I have seen fear control people is through allowing it to create habits of non-action. I have met a number of people who say they don't want to ruin their horse, so they choose to do nothing when their horse presents them with behaviors they don't like. When we stop ourselves from taking action and remain within our comfort zones, we can never reach our true potential.

We need to realize that the same thing happens in our lives, as it does with our horses, when we choose to do nothing rather than something, it is due to fear. In truth, we potentially create more problems through non-action than we are likely to create by taking action. When we find ourselves feeling like it is better to do nothing, it is a sign for us to seek help to educate us on exactly what to do to move forward. Turn your thoughts of non-action into action.

One of the best ways to show this is by discussing unhealthy relationships where we feel stuck and often remain in them for years beyond the time we should have left. People remain in bad relationships for so many reasons, but the negative judgment of others can be high on the list of reasons why. Unfortunately, the judgment can come from those closest to us and this is what makes it so difficult.

Have you ever been in a conversation with someone and heard them say things like, "He was a great guy! I don't know why she left him. She was lucky to have him. She won't find anything better." Or how about, "She has four kids, what is she thinking? She is so selfish. She should have waited until they were done high school at least." Or one of the best I heard, "She is an idiot, he is a great guy. I really like him." These sorts of comments are thoughtless and baseline. To disregard the gravity of someone choosing to leave their spouse by simply stating a basic impression of them is insulting and shows a lack of compassion and one's ability to take on perspective. Bumping into someone on the street and having an eight-minute conversation or seeing someone in a social environment once a week with friends or family does not mean that anyone can judge what they are like as a romantic partner, husband, wife, or otherwise.

It is so easy to make an overall impression of someone based on small snapshots of their personality, but it is not accurate, and it is not appropriate to use those impressions as our opinion whether someone should or should not stay married to them. Not every person decides to end a relationship because they believe the other person is an awful person, they may very well be just as great as people perceive them, but that does not mean that they are perfect for the person who they decided to spend the rest of their life with. We don't know the struggles people have, and we should not assume we know enough about the ins and outs of someone's marriage based on any time spent with them to pass judgment.

Life is far more complex to narrow down whether something is good, bad, or ugly for someone else based on an impression given to us by moments in time. The best we can do when we see that someone has made a choice that contradicts our views, such as leaving a spouse we think is a great person, is to understand that perspective is everything. Keep in mind, some fake flowers are so well made it is very difficult to see that they are indeed fake from a distance, it is not until you get up close and personal and get to *feel* them that you can see that they deceived you all this time.

When we respond to other's choices without empathy or perspective, then we can place doubt in their mind even after they have spent more time then we can fathom making the decision they finally dared to tell us. Thoughts of making any big life change, such as leaving a spouse, comes with moments of absolute sureness and then halting doubt. We should support our friends and loved ones by responding empathetically toward their situation in conversations with them, and in conversations we may have *about* them. We must listen and respond to our friends and loved ones consciously, support them by helping them work through their thoughts, and not judge them. When our responses come from a place of judgment, we feed self-doubt.

When we listen to self-doubt and the doubt of others, we

limit the risks we take. We keep ourselves small and our lives stagnant. When we question whether we should do something we often perceive the action as risky. Risks are defined differently by everyone. People determine risk based on their life experiences, and their personality. Some people only think of life-threatening actions as risks such as skydiving, race car driving, or anything that involves almost certain death if something were to go wrong. To others, however, walking out their front door every morning could feel like a risk. One does not make the other any less courageous or strong; it is all how we perceive our environment and how it will potentially affect us.

It is important for us to understand where we each stand in the assessment of risk and how it influences our daily decision making. I am no daredevil. I often find myself saying no to things because with a quick, automatic, and almost unconscious assessment I deem them unsafe. Or as I tell myself, unnecessary. That being said, I have learned to take my initial reaction as a small caution. I try not to allow it to make my final decision though. I am learning to say yes more and have gained confidence in doing so. I am now aware that taking no risks at all can cause just as much, if not more, damage than taking the biggest ones we can imagine.

By continually limiting our risk-taking we always tell ourselves we can't, shouldn't, and won't. When we embrace risk, no matter how small, we repeatedly tell ourselves we can, should, and will. In doing so, we consciously shift our internal dialog to empowering language which comes out in what we do and what we say. When we push through fear, we open up to conscious communication, which is vulnerable, empathetic, and authentic. We will never be free from fear, but we can become so clear in our communication with ourselves that we will know when it is true fear, the kind that will keep us safe, or an ego-based fear, which will keep us playing small and preventing us from experiencing the joy we deserve.

When we allow fear to overpower our decisions, we operate

from a place that is not genuine with who we are. Instead, we make decisions based on the fear of what others might think, what might result, and what might not happen. We already discussed where "mights" get us! We spend our time doubting more than doing and our communication with ourselves and others becomes unclear. We know that great relationships are built on trust and respect, how do we trust and respect others when we do not trust and respect ourselves? And better yet, how do we set boundaries and share our vulnerabilities if we are ruled by fear? We cannot.

Doubt does not leave room for presence. When we are not present, we cannot perform or communicate to the best of our ability. It is a Catch-22. We don't want to make mistakes or be judged, yet we allow the preconceived judgment and negative internal dialog to stop us from working to the best of our ability and in turn we reaffirm all of our negative thoughts. We get so wrapped up in doubting our abilities, fear of doing something wrong, or having someone negatively judge us, that as a result, we are incapable in that moment of doing anything to our potential.

With horses, doubt changes our timing, our pressure, our ability to be soft, and our energy. Doubt and fear stop us from working in accordance with our intentions because we are focused on the wrong thing. If we silence our inner doubt and negative inner dialog we will perform to the best of our ability. There would be less need for fear of judgment or mistakes because we would be doing the best we could do. How could we get any better than that and how can someone really judge us when that happens—wait, they will still judge us, but what will their judgment matter? Their judgment is on them. It is something they need to work through; it is not our problem.

Furthermore, when we push through doubt, and we become present in all that we do and do it to the best of our ability, we may inspire someone else. If we invested the same amount of energy into being proud of ourselves, being sure of our actions, and focusing on the positive impact that we could have on others as we do doubting and fearing, we would feel our confidence soar to a level we have yet to experience, and we will help others by doing it. We always seem to notice when others are seeing us in a negative way, yet we never seem to know when someone is looking at us as a role model, a leader, or an inspiration to push past their own doubt.

When we work with horses, we spend a lot of time teaching them to be confident in situations which they would naturally want to run away from. We work through their fears by showing them that we can be trusted and what they fear is not going to hurt them. My husband and I spend weekends teaching people how to navigate through obstacles which our riders perceive as scary. What really happens is we work through the riders' fears to show them how to communicate in a way that has their horse looking to them for answers when they are unsure of a situation, rather than taking matters into their own "hands." The result is people who learn to communicate clearly despite their fear, and this allows them to have success where they never thought they could. I wish people would approach their own lives the same way they approach our trail clinics; with excitement and anticipation. They look at the obstacles before them, and through guidance and encouragement, they become present and deal with what is presented to them in a conscious manner, which gets them over the obstacle and excited to tackle the next.

So, what stops us from consciously working through our fears, no matter how big or small? At times we may feel like we are living lives we have no control over, that our job is not what we want, our husband or wife does not give us what we need, and our friends don't act like friends. We may believe that is *just* life, and if that is what is present then that is what we have to live with; this is not true. We are responsible for the direction of our lives, external factors most definitely have an influence, but we often find comfort in our suffering. Taking responsibility and control of our lives is often so overwhelming that remaining stagnant feels like the only choice available.

Fear can hold us back from so many choices in our lives. From small decisions to large life choices. Fear stops us from doing things like speaking to someone new, taking a dance class alone, taking that trip we've always wanted, leaving our abusive partner, or leaving our job we find little to no joy in. Every decision we make, large or small, all have an impact on our lives, although it is not this impact we tend to fear. The fear I see that holds people back most often is the fear of what others will think. *What if others laugh at me? What if others don't understand why I am doing it? What if others think I shouldn't? What if others judge me? What if people see me fail?* We spend so much time fearing what other people think; we don't allow ourselves to think about the positives our decisions could bring into our lives. When did we start believing the opinion or judgment of others was more important than our own happiness, growth, and freedom? This may be easier said than done, but I promise it is possible. We have to start making decisions that are based on self-love and self-awareness and understand the judgment of others is a reflection of them, not us.

When we are able to move beyond the judgment of others, we find a new sense of freedom. In saying this, I think it is important to note that I am not talking about the defensive manner people say, "I don't give a shit what people think of me." When we speak in this way, it is a reflection of a barrier we have put up to shut people out. I have witnessed a lot of people who present themselves with an assertive "I don't care" manner who actually care a whole lot. They use this attitude to try to stop people from seeing their vulnerabilities. When we truly come to a point in life where we are less concerned about the opinion of others, it comes about as a more internal realization which is shown through action more so than with words. When we begin to love ourselves enough to let go of the judgment of others, we will be able to make choices which lead to our happiness more often. When we begin to live a brave life, the judgment of others can still hurt, but with less influence over us. We can choose thoughts that serve us rather than scare us.

When I hear people tell us we need to "control our thoughts," it reminds me of someone telling another that they "need to control their emotions," or that they are "too emotional," or "too sensitive." We need not concern ourselves with *controlling* our thoughts. We are not in a battle with our mind where we need to handcuff all the negative thoughts we have, chain them in the corner, and pretend they aren't there. If we feel the need to *control* them, we will live feeling like we have something to hide. We will know we have merely locked something up to starve rather than taking them by the hand, walking them into the sun, and letting the light sink in.

There is no healing in confinement. Healing comes when we free ourselves from negativity. Not concealing and denying it. It is vital that we educate ourselves and our kids that "*When you mask your feelings, you mask your soul. Furthermore, you inhibit your soul from evolving into its full potential—the chance to really live, to find truth, and to accept it.*"[29]

The key is to *consciously choose* to shift our thoughts in a more loving direction. One thought at a time. We can use our thoughts to understand ourselves, forgive ourselves, and love ourselves, which opens the door to offer the same to others.

When we feel negative thoughts and emotions, there is no room for fear or shame. Those thoughts are just as important as all of our positive ones. When we catch ourselves in a negative state, whether that be a flood of destructive thoughts or just a feeling of slight discontentment, we must use it to snap us back into the present. We cannot lose patience with ourselves and meet them with frustration or anger; rather we need to use them as an opportunity to reflect on what is occurring at that time. Is the feeling being induced by worry about something coming up in the future? Is it guilt from the past? Is it an unsureness of the present? All of these feelings can be shifted to a more loving place by bringing ourselves back into the present moment. If we use our feelings to tell us which way to turn in life, we will go in a much more aligned direction with who we truly are. We should not mask our feelings and look at them as something that holds us back. We need to use them to propel us forward toward love.

While writing this book I was told some people doubted me or mocked my decision to write a book. Little did they know I have always dreamed of becoming a writer. I allowed myself to feel sad over their remarks. I even allowed myself time to cry over it. Then I pulled myself together with a cup of tea and a better perspective. I called someone who made me smile, and I reminded myself of something Oprah once said in an interview: *"You cannot live a brave life without disappointing some people."*[30] This is true, but it will still feel awful. Rather than have it change our mind, it needs to change our perspective. There have been a few specific times in my life that the doubt of others fueled my fire and pushed me to continue during the times when I thought I should give up.

One particular instance comes to mind for me. It was one of the first times I spoke to someone outside of my close-knit circle about writing this book. I had a picture of how these sorts of conversations would go, "So, I hear you are writing a book!" to which I would excitedly respond, "I am!" I would be met with some array of supportive response, like, "Great!" "Impressive" or even a half-hearted, "Good for you." The beginning of this conversation started just as I had imagined, and then they added a word at the end that totally caught me off guard and made me want to hide. The gentlemen, one who I considered a friend, approached me and said, "So I hear you are writing a book. *Really?*" I tried to hide my hurt and played it off like I didn't hear the condescending "really" and moved on from the subject.

Months later, I was still writing, and I thought of that awful question every time I wanted to quit. Some days it would slip in as a voice of doubt, and I heard the *really* whisper in my ear, and then I would respond with a proud, *really*!

I now smile when I see this man. I silently thank him for motivating me through the times I thought I couldn't or shouldn't. His voice will likely continue to push me in times of doubt because of the feeling of empowerment we gain when we prove someone wrong about their perceived limitations of us and being able to accomplish things despite the doubt of others. I try to keep in mind; their doubt is their own demon, not mine. It is often a reflection of something they would not think is worth the risk to them or something they would be able to accomplish.

Making choices to change our life for the better comes in many forms, from deciding to adopt, moving to a new town or country, leaving a partner with a long history, or it could be as small as deciding to ask someone out to dinner. All of the choices we make in our own best interest have the possibility of being very frightening but can also be very rewarding.

Deciding to leave my full-time career was no easy task. It did not come without hours of self-doubt and doubt expressed freely from those around me. When I first had what I called "the crazy thought" of leaving teaching I pushed it out of my mind immediately. Within seconds I had a flash of fear from all the "what ifs" that made me dismiss the idea and think it was impossible.

The problem is when your heart finally speaks, and you take a second to listen to it, you can't "unhear" it. Even if it's a split second, the desire will not leave quite that easily, no matter how crazy you think it is. Each time it popped into my head I gave it a little more recognition and a little more time to resonate in my mind. It didn't feel any less crazy at first.

When I began having the courage to say it out loud, I always lead into the conversation with, "I know this sounds crazy, but . . ." However, I began allowing myself the time to feel and understand where my desire to create such a huge change in my life was coming from. I started rationally assessing the idea. Was it really as crazy as I initially thought? If not, why did my brain shut it down so quickly? There is only one answer to this: *fear*.

I distinctly remember the day I officially decided that I was going to go through with it. My sister had recently moved less than two minutes from my home, so I grabbed tea for us at the drive-thru and headed over with the intent to finally vocalize my decision and talk it through with someone who knew me, knew my situation, and knew that I was in a place where I desired change. We sat on her spare bed while our daughters played and I let the words leave my mouth. I used her as a sounding board for my thoughts and could hear myself bouncing back and forth between what I desired and what I feared.

In the midst of the conversation, I had to leave the room for some menial task and brought my phone with me. While I was gone from our conversation, the universe stepped in. I received a notification that Jennifer Jayde, an inspiring life coach I had begun following, was doing a live video. I clicked on it and felt as though she was speaking directly to me. Jennifer said she only had a few minutes, but she had felt a nudge to share something with her followers. I am self-aware enough to know that it was not only me who needed to hear this, the timing though was absolutely vital for me in my decision-making process.

Jennifer began speaking as if she was a part of my conversation with my sister. In fact, if I had of taken the words from her live video and inserted them into our conversation, it would have been the exact feedback I needed at the exact time I needed it. Jennifer spoke of the almost debilitating fear she experienced when she first decided to leave her nine-to-five job for a life that was more aligned with her. She spoke of being torn between doing the right thing, listening to her heart, and where that might take her, and the thoughts that she was being totally unrealistic, and should just be more grateful for the job and life she already had. She then went on to explain fear and the biological need for the fear response in our bodies and how often it gets triggered at times when we should push through it because it is our heads controlling our decision making rather than our hearts.

There is a saying by Alfred Adler which states, *"Follow your heart, but bring your brain with you."* This perfectly described the process I was going through. It is important when making any decision at all, and especially the ones that make you a little sick and excited all at the same time. Jennifer perfectly explained how to tell the difference between your heart and your head talking. I quickly discovered that my head was filled with so much fear that my heart was only the sound of a whisper. When I turned down the chatter in my head, I was able to hear myself singing that we had found the answer.

As I processed the truth of my desires, I began to have more questions. For me, the biggest question was why did I become a teacher? I had a number of answers flow from pen to paper one day as I journaled: I became a teacher because I did not know how else to create a career out of what I excelled at and neither did any of the people who were helping to guide me. I found myself questioning what happens when we only focus our time and energy on what others think is right for us and never take the time to question if it is truly right for us. I wondered how many people would take a brave leap later in life. I wondered if some will have their dreams and desires smothered until they are completely burned out.

One day while cleaning stalls, my therapy, I was listening to Mike Dooley's audiobook, *Leveraging the Universe*. Out of everything he said one thing, in particular, stood out to me. He spoke of people who spend more time reacting to their life than deliberately creating it.[31] This is profound. For the first time in my conscious memory, I was deliberately creating the life I wanted to live. Even though I am blessed with a wonderful family, a beautiful home, and a career I spent years becoming educated for, I didn't feel like any of those were results of deliberate actions. They were obviously desires I had that then came to be, yet I did not make the conscious decision to *create* anything.

Let me explain. My involvement in horses, for instance, did not happen because I decided after much deliberation that I loved them and wanted to learn to ride. I did not deliberately invite them into my life, the decision was made for me, and my passion grew from there.

When I was seven years old and my sister, Lisa, was nine, my grandfather, who was a jockey in his younger years, suggested to my mom and dad that they buy us a pony. Fast forward through their deliberation, we were soon after welcoming a beautiful gray pony into the family named Ripple. That decision my parents made on my behalf shaped the lives of myself and my two sisters. We grew up competing heavily and learning skills and values that came with the responsibility of owning horses and being in a competitive sport. I then married a man whose passion for horses surpassed my own when we met. His passion drove mine further as we delved into a business that harnessed our knowledge and gave a perfect platform for us to share it with others. I am grateful for my parents' decision to make a life with horses a reality for me and not just a little girl's dream, despite me not directly choosing it for myself.

Another example is my path resulting in me becoming a teacher. Now, of course, I personally made choices along each road I have taken, but those felt like side roads; I don't feel like I ever chose a major highway, so to speak.

My first year of university I pushed back against what my parents wanted me to do, and I went to a small university in the city. My family would have preferred that I go to a quaint university in a beautiful town thirty minutes from home. My decision to attend a different university was a result of a couple of factors. Firstly, I was told someone doubted my ability to complete the course I enrolled in. They were under the impression I was not intelligent enough. So, in tune with my character, hearing this motivated me to go and prove them otherwise, rather than allow their doubt to prompt and increase my own. I used it as motivation. Secondly, I wasn't entirely sure I wanted to go to university at all. Without the approval of my parents to take a year off, I chose to attend a university they did not promote. This choice made me feel like I was slightly in control, even though the decision was not made as a result of knowing what I wanted to do.

I still felt like I was out of tune with my path in university at the end of my first year. After the first year, I chose to submit and go to the university recommended by my parents. The next three years I completed courses that put me to sleep, with the odd professor who seemed to spark just enough in me to keep me going. I started dating someone in the later years of my degree who was on the path to become a teacher, and that seemed to answer my questions. As a teacher, I would likely find success because I was good at school, loved kids, had experience teaching, and I wouldn't disappoint my family.

My future was decided just like that. I did not take time to think about what I truly wanted to do for the rest of my life. I let the decision happen as a result of the opinion of others, a lack of personal research, and fear. Despite this, I invested myself in teaching 100%. I was good at it because I committed to it and I enjoyed connecting with my students. I will always teach, and I will use the lessons I learned from all of my experience in the classroom. I am thankful for the path I was set on, and I am thrilled now to begin to make choices that allow me to deliberately create my life now rather than react to it.

While I was going through the process of accepting my intention to leave my full-time teaching job, the book *The 5 Second Rule* by Mel Robbins was recommended to me. It was exactly what I needed to hear, exactly when I needed it. I used Robbins' method of counting down to take action and propel me to do something that I was terrified to do, but something I knew was absolutely necessary.

It was not long after telling my husband my final decision that I saw two of my administrators talking in the hall while I was walking up to the lunchroom. I counted down, and when I approached them, I simply said, "Do you have about seven minutes to talk at the beginning of next class?" I knew this was not the time or place, so I used the situation to allow me to take a small action that committed me to take further, larger action later. You may wonder, why seven minutes? Why not the regular five or ten-minute requests? Well, I have created a habit of asking people for seven because I know five will not do my request justice, but ten is likely more then I need. It also makes them curious about why I said seven and creates a quick interest in what I said versus hearing me need their time.

So often we know we need to do something specific to make a change, whether that be a shift in our relationship with an awkward conversation or a shift in our job with a request for a raise or more flexible hours. Whatever it is, we all know when we need to do it. It is pushing past the excuses to make it happen that is important. There will always be excuses not to. *Always.* We have to want our own happiness so badly that no excuse is good enough.

This is where we get the chance to actively create our lives. I could have seen my administrators standing on their lunch break and thought that it was not the time and place to have this conversation and that I'd find them later, but I guarantee I would not have. It would have taken a few more days or weeks for a situation to line up for the perfect timing for the conversation. By then I likely would have talked myself out of the decision altogether due to fear, or just come up with another excuse for it to happen later. I needed to set up my opportunity to bite the bullet at that very moment because it was at that moment that my intuition was talking to me. I needed to listen to it before my brain interrupted.

In Mel Robbins' book, she offers scientific research that explains *The 5 Second Rule* and why it works. If you haven't read it, I highly suggest it.[32] I appreciate all the science that backs up this method of approaching decision making, but I appreciate the results I experienced personally even more. I will explain the concept very briefly and try to make it as simple as it is. Essentially, when we think of something that requires us to act, to say something, or to do something, countdown: 5-4-3-2-1. Then you do it. Robbins talks about how this shifts our brain and creates new patterns and breaks habits and, in turn, changes our lives. The moment I saw my administrators standing together my heart nudged me to take action. I counted down as I approached them and then I spoke. What Robbins' method took away was hesitation, and the time it would take for my brain to convince me I should wait for another time.

The next thing I discovered was that, while *The 5 Second Rule* helped me take action, it did not take away my fear once the action was taken. This is where I discovered that with every large decision I would have to think and act on, there were many small and equally scary decisions to get to the end. *The 5 Second Rule* does not come in handy only once per decision, but possibly multiple times. I walked away from my coworkers feeling slightly exhilarated, yet absolutely sick to my stomach. My ego jumped in as I climbed the stairs and began to fill my head with worry and doubt.

It was only due to the coaching course I was enrolled in at the time that I knew it was my ego talking. I needed to hear the worry and to release it. In the past, I would have probably felt the anxiety attached to my brave and *stupid* step and would have emailed them to lie and tell them that I was having a computer issue and it was resolved. Rather than becoming overwhelmed with self-doubt, I acknowledged my feelings and carried on with my lunch. I did not allow my mind to get carried away with worry and interrupt my time in the day that I got to laugh with my colleagues and enjoy a break.

Lunch ended, and I used the bell as my catalyst. I got up knowing what I had arranged to do and went to my class to take a breath then walked downstairs. I knew if I stopped to talk to anyone I would likely falter. So I smiled and nodded but did not stop. I approached my principal's office and took the leap. I told him I needed to create flexibility in my life and that I would not be returning to my full-time contract in September. My voice was shaking, and I held back every emotion the best I could. I respected my principal greatly, he had given me the opportunity to be in the position I was in and I was so nervous I would disappoint him or make him feel unappreciated. His response put my soul at ease. The first thing he said was, "Congratulations." His reaction was unexpected and refreshing. I felt the tension leave my body and I settled into the conversation.

I left his office feeling lighter, but as I made my way back to my classroom, I began to feel panic sink in again. My brain was trying to interfere and send me back downstairs to reverse my decision. I knew why I felt this way and kept repeating to myself that it was going to be okay. It was part of the plan.

I am hardwired, as are you, to fear change. My brain was trying to protect me. It was up to me to push past the fear and stay true to the course my heart had set me on. In the past, I would have misunderstood my emotional reactions and likely misread them. I would have listened to my fear because that is what we do and then I would be stuck in the same place, doing the same thing, feeling the same feelings of discontent, lack of motivation, frustration, and guilt. If I did not consciously push through my fear and past the walls of my comfort zone, I would never feel what I desired: peace, purpose, excitement, and fulfillment.

Exercise:

Do you have any decision that you have been pushing out of your mind? Big or small? I want to motivate you to push yourself to begin making decisions based on your heart rather than always your head. The same as I learned from Jennifer Jayde. I want you to begin to take your thoughts and dreams seriously and turn them into action in your life rather than dismissing them as "silly," "impossible," or "too risky." I am not saying to take uncalculated and dangerous risks all of a sudden. I am encouraging you to really listen to yourself and take action which may feel scary, but also may bring you more joy.

So, how do we do this? How do you tell when it is your heart versus your head talking? It was first made clear to me by Jennifer when she explained that your initial answer to a thought or idea is usually your heart. So, for instance, someone older asks you to go on a date, your first thought is, "YES!", then your head steps in and you hear, "But, what if?" The "what if" could be a number of things: What if my dad doesn't approve? What if people talk because of our age difference? What if he has kids/his ex-wife finds out I'm younger/I end up really liking him/he isn't right for me? All of the questions, mostly ones that result from a fear of judgment, all stop you from making decisions based on your heart. Your head tries to keep you safe. Your heart tries to keep you alive.

If something excites you and scares you at the same time, it may just be exactly what you need to do.

Next, grab your journal and pen to begin the exercise. This one may be something you go back and add to whenever something comes up, but right now try to add at least 10 things to your list.

You are going to write a bucket list. Not any bucket list though, your heart list. On this list I want you to set down your fears; fears of judgment, fears of emotional hurt, or anything else that has limited your decision making in the past. What do you want to do in this life?

For me, one of my items on my heart list has always been to write a book. I have started many over the years and never saw any to the finish, or even middle since we are being honest. I knew my heart wanted to write a book, but it wasn't into the topics I had chosen in the past. They felt forced and out of touch.

I began this particular book at 2:00 a.m. with a single thought running through my mind over and over, *"You approached it like it was heavy, so it was."* I rolled over, trying not to wake my husband, and opened the notes app on my phone. That was the first line I wrote, and the rest seemed to take shape around it. I could not stop thinking about it. It was pouring from my soul. I wrote and wrote and wrote. Then I began to doubt. I heard comments from people around me, the naysayers.

I took a few months off before finishing because I began to listen to my head, the voice of doubt made a significant impact on my confidence versus my heart which knew this book could help at least one person. That being said, I think it is important to admit that throughout the time I was not writing, even though I was so close to being finished, if anyone asked me why I wasn't writing at the time I would have given every excuse in the book, no pun intended, other than fear. I would have told them that I was too "busy"—a word we use as a filler for things like scared, intimidated, feeling doubtful. I was too busy doing anything other than writing. Now don't get me wrong, what I busied myself with was worth every second but none of it, other than time with my husband and daughter, was more important than accomplishing my dream. I almost allowed others' doubts to take away an opportunity to feel the satisfaction of checking off my biggest "to-do" ever.

Through a small kick in the ass by some very supportive people, I decided to kick back into gear and finish what I had started. I saw the impact of what negativity can do to us. I allowed the doubt of only a few people overshadow the support of *so* many. As Jennifer taught me, I needed to remove the paper from my face. While discussing my fear of committing to big decisions because of the potential adverse judgment of others, Jennifer said something to me during a coaching call that has helped me through many situations since. She told me to place a small black dot in the center of a piece of white paper and to hold the paper up with the dot to my eye. She asked me what I would see if I did this. Clearly, I said the black dot. She then told me to remove the paper from my face and asked me how what I saw had changed. This was the first time I was able to change my perspective in regard to the amount of judgmental versus supportive people I had in my world. Why was I focusing on that small black dot when there was so much clean white space? You see, when we look at situations where we only focus on the negatives, all we see is the black, and we miss the positive that surrounds it.

Write your list as if the possibility of judgment or failure is impossible and non-existent. I want you to dream big and be sure to dream for you, not anyone else!

Here are some of my items on my current heart list (heart lists are subject to change, just as you are):

1. Finish this book (If you are reading this, CHECK!)

2. Meet Brené Brown

3. Record an audiobook

4. Cultivate a circle of friends who seek to understand, inspire, and love

5. Empower women through my work

6. Continue to advance my horsemanship

7. Meet Oprah Winfrey

8. Show my daughter how to live with love and passion

9. Present a Ted Talk

10. Change a stranger's life

11. Go on a cattle drive with my husband and daughter

12. Bring like-minded women together

13. Ride a racehorse

14. Ride a professional's cutting horse

15. Drink Tim Horton's tea with my friend Izzy (I was able to check this off while writing, but it will always remain on my list).

16. Age gracefully

This is not my complete list and my list changes on a regular basis. Remember this list is not a 100% commitment. It is what your heart wants at the present moment. That could change at any time based on experience and personal growth. The important part is to really tap into what you desire to experience in life based on the positive feelings you feel these items will bring. Oh, and have fun with it and leave fear behind!

In addition to your heart list, please begin using *The 5 Second Rule* when you know you need a little or a big push. You will not regret using this strategy to eliminate excuses and take necessary action in your life.

CHAPTER EIGHT

Stepping Away from Drama

"We all need someone who inspires us to
be better than we know how."

Unknown

I thought I was almost finished writing this book when I took part in a clinic with Andrea Anderson of Higher Horsemanship. As it turns out, I was just getting started. This chapter and the next are a direct result of the lessons I learned throughout the clinic. As Andrea spoke, I had spark after spark of inspiration. It was as if she knew the book I was writing and was talking to me directly, even though she was speaking to an intimate group of several horse enthusiasts without a clue that she was connecting so many dots for me. As Andrea addressed issues with our horses, she seamlessly and unconsciously connected them to human communication and connection. Everything she said spoke to my soul and made me reflect further on my own horsemanship practices and communication overall. She became a major influence on how I would continue my book and my work with horses.

Andrea taught the most empathetic form of horsemanship I had ever witnessed. She shook me to the core when she allowed me to discover that I could be so much more, and in this case less was more. Less pressure, less drama, less excuses, all resulted in more clear communication and an approach in tune with everything I wanted my horsemanship to be.

Andrea allowed me to dig deeper into how I communicated with my horse and it allowed me to reflect more on how I was communicating with my husband, my daughter, my friends, and everyone else. She taught me how to communicate from a place of empathy beyond what I thought was possible. She was exactly the person I needed to meet before finishing this book because she gave me the feedback I needed personally to bring my communication to another level and bring further insight into my writing. By the end of the clinic, I referred to Andrea as "the Brené Brown of horsemanship." As you continue reading, I hope you will see why.

On the first day of the clinic I had my first big aha moment with one simple, yet so complex, statement from Andrea. She was asking a horse to do something for the first time and when he finally found the correct response to her pressure she eloquently said, "Now, I want him to sit and think about what he has done right." This statement was a life changer for me. Coming from a profession in education and having a young daughter, these words felt like a slap in the face, but the sting woke me up to a whole new level of conscious communication.

"Think about what they've done right."

When Andrea said this, I learned that we must handle our horses with empathy and open doors for them to make the right choices rather than focus on shutting doors to prevent actions or responses we do not desire. She taught me to change my reaction when a horse offers me a different response than what I am looking for. Everything Andrea said during the clinic translated from my relationships with my horses to the relationships I have with people.

I began thinking about this concept when I was working through difficult situations with my daughter; she is a strong-willed and intelligent little girl. Before I met Andrea, when my daughter did something she knew better than to do, I would send her to timeout. As most of us think the purpose of a timeout is, I would expect her to think about what she had done wrong. I never took deliberate time to have to think about and reinforce when I saw her do the right things, only the wrong things. I knew I would still have to maintain my routine when she did not behave; however, I needed to be sure I was encouraging her to think just as much, if not more, about what she did right as well.

We seem to only offer our most concentrated attention to our children when they are doing the wrong things. It is no wonder they tend to repeat negative behaviors. Kids *need* our attention. They will do what they can to get it, even if that means misbehaving. If we want our kids to grow up to be confident, caring, good citizens, we should spend more time focusing on the good they do rather than the bad. We all reinforce good behaviors, whether it be a pat on the neck of our horse or a soft word to our child. Rarely do I see people use time to think as positive reinforcement. We offer a quick "good job" and move on, yet we use thinking time to try to change negative behaviors.

When we release pressure from a horse, we teach them what we are looking for. They need time to think and process their choice. I believe children do as well. If nothing else, the time we take to have them think about what they have done right will be a positive time being in their own minds. We want our children to be content to be with their own thoughts and not need constant stimulus or entertainment. If we only ever force them to take time to "sit and think" about what they have done wrong, it is not difficult to foresee that when they have isolated time to think, they could form negative thinking patterns as a result. We do not all form negative thought patterns in the same way. Nevertheless, I think we all know that negative thought patterns can be destructive. If we can prevent them from developing in our children by changing our perspective and our communication, I think it is worth it.

As a former classroom teacher, I saw an increase in the number of students who came to me confiding that they suffered from depression and anxiety. These students were medicated, not writing tests, not writing exams, being excused from class presentations, and sometimes leaving school altogether. The increase in the number of students who were being medically excused from writing exams was the first thing to really set me back and got me thinking about what is happening to our youth and the messages that we are sending them. Most importantly the messages they are sending themselves. They are riddled with "I can't," and "I won't," and frozen in fear of failure and judgment. I don't believe that letting them off the hook for these things is the answer. I think they truly do feel like they can't and forcing them to do these things in their mental state will not help them in the long run; they need to learn to change their inner dialog.

I don't believe having a doctor help teens with anxiety is a bad thing. Do not get me wrong; there is always an appropriate time for different measures, from notes excusing specific tasks to the prescription of medication. On the other hand, I also believe that we must teach our children and teens that fear and stress are not something to try to avoid at all costs or to run away and hide from. Life is made up of so many triggers for us, and the desire to live happily is ideal, but the idea that we can only be happy by eliminating things that cause us any form of anxiety is unrealistic and unhealthy. We need to teach our teens that it is okay to feel anxious at times and accomplishing important tasks proves to ourselves that we are capable.

Every situation is individual, and I know it is at this point some parents will read this and feel the need to email me their defense of why their child was or is a special case. Believe me when I say, I get it. I have a daughter. I will want to protect her, but not at all costs. I cannot protect her at the cost of personal growth and coping skills. I cannot protect her so much so that she does not develop important traits that lead to success such as resilience, drive, grit, determination, confidence, perseverance, and faith.

It is important that we teach our children, and perhaps firstly, ourselves, that our emotions are not to be feared, avoided, and pushed down. We must use our emotions to show us where to go, not where *not* to go. Our emotions can guide us if we let them. Rather than feeling negative emotions and running from them, it is important that we allow them to tune us into what our triggers are, reflect on them, and work through them.

When we teach our children to think in a healthy way, eat in a healthy way, or move in a healthy way, it is essential to teach them to do so for one simple reason: To be healthy. Not to fit in, not to be thin, not to be less of who they are in any way, shape, or form. It is to become more of who they are. I want my daughter to be compassionate toward herself, not critical. I want to teach her to try to use her mind and body to the best of her ability to make her strong and energetically aligned to optimize her ability to feel joy and happiness as much as possible.

I think we need to be conscious of the messages we send children as young ones and also teach them how to think responsibly from when they are young; dealing with little kid things like sharing all the way through to high school and dealing with peer pressure and self-doubt. We have to encourage and teach safe thinking the same as we do sex, and drinking and driving in their teen years because their thoughts are just as, if not more so, potentially dangerous. We should teach them that, as stated on Psychology Today by writer Hara Estroff Marano: *". . . negative thinking slips into the <u>brain</u> under the radar of conscious awareness and becomes one of the strongest of habit patterns. People generate negative thoughts so automatically they are unaware that it is happening, that it is actually a choice they are making."*[33] Young people need to understand how *"critical the quality of our thinking is to maintaining and even intensifying depression."*[34]

The most efficient way to change how we feel is to change the way we think. We have to teach our children to communicate consciously with themselves, maybe even more so, than how they communicate with others. Think about how much further ahead our children will be if they do not have to change *how* they think to live a happy life instead they learn to think responsibly from the beginning.

Time to think about the positive is crucial for horses and children, and it is just as important for adults going from task to task on their daily grind. As adults, we tend to dwell on our mistakes and the mistakes of others so much that we rob ourselves of positive and healthy internal and external dialog. We get trapped in the cycle of thinking about what we have done wrong and rarely spend time dwelling on how awesome our loved ones or we are.

If you find yourself wrapped up in the negative and rarely swept away by the positive, don't worry, you are just human, it is how we are made. The great thing is, we can change. As humans, we are hardwired to have a stronger reaction to negativity than positivity. This is referred to as "Negativity Bias." We are naturally super sensitive to negativity, and this means negative experiences play a very significant role in every aspect of our lives and it plays a notably powerful role in our most intimate relationships.

In the article, *Our Brain's Negative Bias: Why our brains are more highly attuned to negative news*, Estroff Marano states, *"Numerous researchers have found that there is an ideal balance between negativity and positivity in the atmosphere between partners . . . What really separates contented couples from those in deep marital misery is a healthy balance between their positive and negative feelings and actions toward each other."*[35]

You know those couples who seem to fight like crazy, the ones who scream and shout and argue and people question how they ever stay together? Well, this will help explain it. Those seemingly volatile couples are able to maintain their relationship by balancing their hostility with a lot of love and passion. They don't, however, get to maintain an equal balance between the fighting and the loving. They must have more positive than negative.

According to research, there needs to be a five-to-one ratio to be exact, due to the disproportionate weight negativity has on our brains. According to researchers, this very specific ratio needs to exist between the amount of positivity and negativity to sustain a satisfying married life for both partners. Marano said, *"As long as there was five times as much positive feeling and interaction between husband and wife as there was negative, researchers found, the marriage was likely to be stable over time. In contrast, those couples who were heading for divorce were doing far too little on the positive side to compensate for the growing negativity between them."*[36]

It has been found that similar results occur in other aspects of our lives as well, the frequency of five-to-one small positive acts remain the same. Marano explains further by stating, *"Occasional big positive experiences—say, a birthday bash—are nice. But they don't make the necessary impact on our brain to override the tilt to negativity. It takes frequent small positive experiences to tip the scales toward happiness.*"[37] Likely, there would be some discrepancy based on personality types and compatibility, much like we see with horses. Some are more forgiving than others and some much less forgiving based on their personality and past experiences. I would bet that this ratio of small positives to negatives likely applies to all relationships we keep, human to human or human to horse.

Don't Enter into Their Drama

Not entering into their drama was the second biggest take away I took from Andrea. It changed my perception of how I should handle horses and humans who present behaviors I would have reacted strongly to in the past. I learned the value of maintaining a consistent pressure or presence, as opposed to validating their responses by becoming an active participant in their drama. When we do not enter into another's drama, we teach them that we will remain true to our intent and will not waiver. We will maintain our position and will keep our head about us in the process, by doing so, we communicate to them, "We are not about that," and in turn, they look for a new answer.

When we do not get pulled into our horse's drama, we have the ability to continue to open doors for the right answer versus reprimanding them for choosing the wrong answer. You might be thinking, staying out of others' drama may be easy with horses, but . . .

Know that I understand. Horses don't gossip, they don't intentionally hurt feelings, and they don't cheat on their partner. What *they* do is offer answers which frustrate us, confuse us, and make us wish they would *just* do what we say. Our miscommunications with horses can cause negative emotions in the same way the miscommunications we have with people do. We feel like we lack control over the situation due to someone else's actions and it can be infuriating and sometimes hurtful.

No matter if we are with an animal or a human, when we are feeling anger flood in as a result of someone's actions it takes a fair amount of self-regulation to respond in a way that does not add fuel to the fire. Before we begin to communicate consciously, we allow our thoughts to rule our emotions and we can become wrapped up in drama, especially when it seems to be thrown our way, self-regulation may seem impossible. If not impossible, most undoubtedly unsatisfying. I assure you though, after working through our own emotions and allowing ourselves to maintain our head through miscommunications and drama, it will start to become a habit. Soon, deflecting drama will feel natural and necessary.

That being said, it seems almost natural, and sometimes even necessary, to fall into the drama of others, even when we have become more mindful of our communication. When someone's actions cause us anger, hurt, or frustration it can feel like a direct attack on us as a person. These feelings are often a result of how someone speaks to us or doesn't, or how someone speaks *about* us and we hear about it through the rumor mill. When this occurs for us, we must keep in mind that although it feels like we should defend ourselves, there is strength in remaining silent. Their actions are a result of who they see you as based on their own agenda, not who everyone else sees you as. This form of drama is easy to spot, and we know how damaging it is as we participate in it. However, there is another form of drama that is equally as damaging for us to become involved in but may be a bit trickier to catch ourselves in because it does not hurt us at the moment.

This particular drama does not concern us or even the people we are discussing the issues with. This drama resides in nasty little conversation starters which ease awkward silence and ease our discomfort when we are unsure if someone likes us or not.

I'm talking about *gossip.* You know the conversations I mean, the ones where someone is being spoken about without being there to defend themselves and having no one to do it for them. It is as though questioning the decisions of others and criticizing what others do becomes a neutral ground for others to bitch on and ease their own distress. They don't ever really care what the answers to their questions are, if they did, they would ask the person they are talking about for themselves rather than sit around and be critical of them.

When I chose to leave teaching I heard from many people that I had caused a bit of talk both in and out of the teaching world and that "people" were wondering why I made the decision. Not one of those people made any effort to call or message me to inquire why. They simply found a common topic with someone and expressed concern where the want for gossip actually stood. If their *concern* was the true purpose for people to discuss my decisions behind closed doors, classrooms, cars, and homes, I should have had quite a few people contacting me asking me directly. However, I did not. They jumped on the bandwagon of gossip and drama and left the conversation feeling no less informed or judgmental, I am sure.

So, why do I say being involved in this form of third-party drama is just as bad as being neck deep in our own dramatic situations? It's simple. We don't form genuine, healthy relationships with these people we bitch with because when it comes down to it, we wonder if they are speaking about us the same way they talked about that other person. We do not leave the conversation feeling better about ourselves, or at least we shouldn't. We bring our vibration down by partaking in discussions like these, and it is not going to make us look good in any way.

I very honestly admit I have partaken in many conversations where the person was not there to defend themselves, and we spoke about things based merely on speculation or judgment. I have never walked away from those conversations feeling good. I would, often, leave with a sick feeling in my stomach or question myself about why I didn't stick up for the person or shut the conversation down. In the least, I could have not contributed at all, but I didn't. I took part, and it made me feel gross. Even now, after a lot of self-assessing and work to change my dialog and perspective, I still can get caught in the drama talk, and it makes me feel worse than ever.

It is interesting though; I have done some thinking about why or who I tend to fall into this trap. It usually is with people who I know speak poorly about me when I am absent or that I know don't like me. I let my insecurities do the talking, and I fall into their same patterns of negative talk. I get so mad when I find myself in these situations, and it takes some pretty strong self-awareness at that moment to stop my contribution to the conversation one way or another.

That being said, when I meet someone new that has these negative speaking habits, which I know make me feel uneasy, I tend to be more careful about the information I offer them. I try not to let them too close. I know how important it is for me to surround myself with people who make me a better person. Whether their negative talk comes from a place of their own insecurities or not, which it often does, I have to be careful not to get too invested in them. This may sound selfish, and it is. It is one of the selfish taking care of "me" habits I formed when I became a more conscious communicator with myself and others.

When we become conscious of not entering into drama, we expose our habits of how we communicate in times of pressure, stress, or increased emotion. Becoming conscious of our poor communication habits allows us to change them, and this is where we have an opportunity to shine our light inward and discover what our own language looks like. It is in this place of conscious communication that we can discover how we speak to ourselves. It is here we have the opportunity and ability to change destructive and negative thought patterns. We cannot change when we are still caught in others' drama because we cannot change our perspective and approach when we are still looking to find blame rather than responsibility. When we change our habits and operate from a place of empathy and compassion, we enter into a growth mindset.

In an online course I took from Eckhart Tolle, I learned to be the thinker, not the thoughts. I have interpreted this to mean that I know who I am and what I am, my thoughts do not make me doubt this. One thought of "I am so dumb," does not mean I actually believe I am dumb at that moment. Just because I think it, does not mean it is true. I discovered through mindfulness and presence that I could listen to my inner voice and change any negative thought patterns I had formed. I am now capable of interrupting a negative thought, very similarly to how I would shut down a conversation which was not serving anyone. I would acknowledge it, then think above it with a new and healthier perspective. I was able to hear my own bullshit and confront it. I didn't confront it in a combative way. I simply found my authentic voice which was not formed by the thoughts and feelings of others and allowed it to communicate beyond my insecurities, judgments, and quick temper. In doing so, I learned how to not enter into my own drama, which I am sure if you asked my mother, is a big deal!

I recently read the title of an article that used the phrase, "*My anxiety makes me*," in it. I did not continue reading and moved on. Later that day I found that line repeated in my head, something felt wrong about it. The article was likely helpful to those who struggle with anxious thoughts; it would have resonated with them and gave them a voice. However, it caused me concern. When we claim something as our own, we often get comfortable with it and identify with it. We need to be mindful of our words. It seems silly, but it is true. When we use phrases like "my anxiety" to describe our anxious thoughts, it sounds like its own entity. We separate ourselves from it in the sense that we do not control it, it controls us. Interestingly, at the same time, we separate ourselves from it, allowing us to forfeit control. We can get away with using our "anxiety" as a scapegoat.

Everyone experiences anxious thoughts. It is when our thoughts control us that we then no longer just experience anxiety, we *have* it. When we claim to *have* it we invite it into every corner of our lives. What is yours is now your anxiety's. We must notice our language around our feelings, remembering mantras influence our lives, be sure you aren't committed to a destructive mantra. Be aware of when you say or think things like, "I have anxiety," "My anxiety causes me to . . . " "I am an anxious person," "I am a worrier," "I am depressed." Once you become aware of this language you have the ability to change it.

Remember you are the thinker, not the thoughts as Tolle teaches. We give power to our thoughts when we use them as a defense. We give them control. When you hear yourself say, "I have anxiety." Try to correct yourself with: "Sometimes I have anxious thoughts that are hard to change, but I know I can." Change your language to change your life.

Is overcoming debilitating anxiety as simple as this? No, but it is a tool you can use every day to help without the help of anyone else. You can reclaim control.

Interrupting anxious thoughts requires us to be present, much like correcting small behaviors in our horses. When we allow our horse to get away with little behaviors, they build on those and one day they bite our arm, and we say in shock, "Goodness, I don't know why he did that! He has never bitten before!" Unfortunately, we were not present enough to recognize all of the small behaviors which led up to the bite over time. In fact, we may have even had little excuses for allowing those behaviors because our attachment to the animal blurred our perception of the meaning behind their actions.

Take for example, a horse that constantly walks into their

owner's space and nibbles on their shirt. The owner may lightly swat them away, but tell someone at the same time that the horse just really loves them and wants to be with them all the time or that they are just so playful, they need something to do all the time. When actions that are undesirable become excused for one reason or another, they do not make them any less likely to build into a more obvious problem. In fact, it likely causes them to. Our anxious thoughts can snowball the same way.

One little anxious thought left unchecked, unrecognized, or excused will grow. If we are not present and allow our thoughts to run on autopilot, we will not notice when our thoughts create pockets of panic and worry until they eventually build up and overwhelm us, leaving us to feel like they have come out of nowhere.

Recently, I caught myself allowing anxious thoughts to take control. It's not something that happens often, but I was driving and fell into the worrying thoughts about what I needed to do, hadn't done, and should have done. I did not shut them down. I had just hit the highway, leaving town to head on a relatively impromptu trip out of the country for a few days. By taking this trip, I was leaving behind many to-dos, priorities, and my child in the hands of my husband and some valued helpers. I allowed my thoughts to send me into a state of feeling guilt and irresponsibility. I did not respond to my thoughts with the reality of the situation, that I had done all I could. I allowed them to build and take control. In less than five minutes I was snapped back into a mindful state by a pain in my chest and shortness of breath.

I immediately felt the panic begin, and then I consciously told myself I was okay. I stopped my panicked thoughts by beginning to focus on and control my breathing. As I maintained my awareness on my breath, I quickly turned on an audiobook that I knew brought me inspiration, and I changed my focus to the author's voice. She sounded strong and sure. Her words were true and helpful. It seemed to take twice as long to release my panic as it did to let it set in, but it slipped away through deep breaths and healthier thoughts. This method worked well for me. However, it may not be right for everyone. Practice methods of changing your thoughts when they first occur, interrupt them sooner and more frequently to learn what works best for you. This reminds me of a well-known quote by horseman Ray Hunt, *"You need to do less sooner; you're always doing too much, late."*[38] If we can do less sooner, we will feel less overwhelmed, less broken, and more connected.

Once we learn to silence the voices that create unnecessary drama in our own minds we are much more capable of observing the drama of others and remaining separate from it, refraining from participating in it, and seeing it from the perspective of an open mind. This allows us to see that everyone is on their own journey and we can sit with them in support, however, not be affected by them personally.

I believe it is important to note here something I learned about myself recently. I pride myself in having a regularly quiet mind. Yes, sometimes it does run a little wild, but for the most part, it is quiet which allows me to be present, think clearly, and respond consciously. I made the mistake of assuming my quiet mind meant I had a calm mind. I have discovered this is not the case. I purchased a tool to mindfully help my meditation practice. That kind of sounds unnecessary, aren't mindfulness and meditation one and the same? My answer is no. Meditation is a mindful approach to connecting with your soul versus your mind.

I purchased a *Muse Brain-Sensing Headband*, through the use of this tool I could see that although my mind is easily quieted, it takes a conscious effort for me to *calm* it. The Muse Headband brought awareness to my meditation practice that I was missing. I was able to tap further into my mind and body to induce quiet *and* calm by feeling what my mind was doing, not just listening to it.

I will use this new knowledge to ensure that I am able to reach a calm state more regularly throughout my days, not only in a quiet state. This is the next step to releasing myself from my own drama and the effects the drama of others has on me.

I am thankful for what Andrea Anderson taught me about horses, but I am indebted to her for teaching me so much about myself.

Exercise:

The exercise in this chapter is going to focus on your miscommunications and sources of drama. I want you to reflect on your arguments, hurt, anger, or frustrated feelings, gossipy conversations, and judgmental comments to understand your responsibility in each situation and others' role in your miscommunication or drama.

In your journal, place the title, "Miscommunications" or "Drama" at the top. It will be helpful to revisit this page for an extended period of time to see the source of your drama, who and how your fire is fueled, and what responsibility you can take on for each situation. It will take commitment to stick to it. Do the best you can, even if it is only for a week.

On this page, you will place the date at the top of each entry, then record what transpired that day. Your entry for one particular day could be that you had ZERO drama or miscommunications, that sort of entry is just as important as the ones where you pour your heart out and vent all of your emotions.

With these entries, I want you to write what happened, who was involved, what was said, how you responded, and how you feel now that it is done.

Once you are done writing, go back and see if anything you said or did could have changed the situation. Were you overreacting? Did you say something that you regret? Did you feed unnecessary drama or did you shut it down? Did someone else's drama cause you stress?

Next, take note of who else was involved. Are they typically a source of stress for you? Do you have regular miscommunications with them? Does drama seem to surround them? Do you feel they are healthy for you? What role do they play in your life?

Here is a *hypothetical* example for you before you begin. Details will be sparse as it is meant to represent the journal of the individual who experienced it directly and does not need to go into detail to assess their feelings:

December 4

Today started out so well. I felt great waking up. I think my internal dialog is finally starting to change. My very first thought today was, "Gosh, I feel good!" I rolled over, and my little one smiled at me as soon as his eyes opened. Is there any better way to wake up? Anyway, forget the positive now! It seemed as soon as my feet hit the floor I was in for a different day. My cell phone rang before I got out of bed, so I ran to the living room to get it. My stomach sank when I saw who was calling. I sat on the couch before answering. My stepbrother's tone of voice was its usual low, sulky sounding tone and I just KNEW he needed something. He didn't even ask me how anyone was; he just started into his regular vent session about how shitty his boss was because he laid him off before Christmas and that he thinks it is because he didn't like how much he was on his phone. He went on and on about how no one is doing anything to help him. All I kept thinking was, and what are you doing to help yourself? So, I said it! I have been holding it in for SO LONG! It just came out before I could stop myself. I was just so frustrated with the same conversation happening again! He hung up immediately. I felt sick! I called my husband to fess up to what I said, and thankfully he understood. He said he would call and fix it because we can't have him mad at us so close to Christmas, he won't get a turkey dinner if he doesn't get one at our house. I instantly felt guilty and agreed that he should try to clear it up, tell him I was PMS-ing or something. GAH! Rob got home at supper and told me he took care of it. He offered him $200, and Josh seemed to forget the whole thing happened. Of course, I could really have used that $200 to help pay off some of my own debt! Three kids this Christmas is way more expensive than I imagined! I'll make it work. I'll pick up an extra shift next week if I can find a sitter.

Reflection:

Was there anything I said or did that could have changed the situation?

Well, yes! But, what I said was the truth! I wasn't mean or anything, I just asked an honest question, and he didn't like what it implied. I could have kept my mouth shut, but I've been doing that now for the last six years.

Was I overreacting?

No, I wasn't when I was on the phone, maybe I was by the time I called Rob though. I probably should have just told him and let it go. I felt awful all day, and for what? Telling the truth? I shouldn't have allowed him to ruin my entire day.

Did I say something I regret?

Yes, and no. I do not regret asking him what he is doing because someone has to try to get him to see he is responsible for his own mess, but I do kind of regret it because now we are $200 poorer, plus sitter money, and another eight hours away from the kids next week. My baby is going to start calling my sitter Mom if I have to keep working this much!

Did I feed unnecessary drama or did I shut it down?

Well, for the first time EVER I stopped him from continuing with his woe is me bull. I guess I shut it down. I have always just listened. I think that is why he always calls me and not his sister because I don't set him straight. She has told me before I am enabling him and it always pissed me off. I thought I was supportive, although I think she was right!

Did someone else's drama cause me stress?

Yes! He made my day terrible when it started out SO GOOD. Wait. I made my day terrible by allowing the situation to control my thoughts and emotions all day. He could have just ruined 10 minutes of my day. Instead, I let him destroy the whole day by being caught in his drama, and then I pulled Rob into it. Got it. It wasn't all his fault. I need to be able to maintain a positive thought process even after something not so positive happens. I get so caught up sometimes, and when I feel guilty for anything, I find it consumes me. Hmmm, this might be a good space in my thought process to use *The 5 Second Rule*.

Who else was involved? Are they typically a source of stress for me?

Josh and YES. Always. I never get off the phone or leave a visit with him feeling better than before we talked.

Do I have regular miscommunications with them?

Sort of, not outwardly though. I normally sit and smile and nod and give the occasional, "Yeah, that's shitty," in response. I always think of the things I should have said once the conversation is over. It is like I get into arguments with myself about him and do nothing about it.

Does drama seem to surround them?

Yes! Always. He is always broke, or fired, or broken up with, and I am always the one he calls.

Do you feel they are healthy for you?

No. They aren't healthy for me, my marriage, or my relationship with anyone involved. I seem to always have arguments with them when his name is involved.

What role do they play in your life?

He is family! I have to continue to be there to support him, don't I? Or do I?

What can you do to help remain out of their drama in the future?

I need to detach from him a bit. I need to make my own mental health a priority. I will speak with him kindly, but I will not engage in the conversation if it becomes negative. I will take a message for my husband and have him call Josh back if he thinks he needs him.

As you can see from this journal entry, a lot of great stuff can come up for you with a little reflection. If I were to chat with this girl, I would suggest she grab this book and pay particular attention to Chapter Six.

CHAPTER NINE

Balance Work and Rest

"My life is joyously balanced with work and play."

Louise Hay

The concept of balancing work and rest with horses is a challenging one to put into practice when we are first learning its importance. The idea that horses are gaining just as much from us when we are allowing them to rest, by not making them move or asking something of them, works against our instinct and ego. The first horseman I had heard this concept from was Jim Anderson, Andrea Anderson's charming husband.

I had gone over twenty years working with horses and had never been told the importance of resting my horse as a way to reinforce what I was teaching them. We like to see things happen. However, when we are resting our horses a lot is taking place on the inside, and the outward signs can be subtle. It takes a trained eye to see and appreciate that. It is not until we let go of the clock and our preconceived notions of what we need to accomplish on a particular day that we can handle our horse in the present.

It is only when we handle our horse in the present that we are able to offer rest when it is truly needed and see the benefits of balancing work and rest. Our horses, with the time to process what was asked of them and where they found their release, tend to look for the answer sooner, more willingly, and with a quieter mind. I believe if we begin to promote an equal balance of work and rest in our human relationships, we will see similar results.

I think it is worth stating that we may want to work to establish this on a personal level before attempting to do so with all of our other relationships. We will never be able to have a perfect balance of work and rest. Realistically not very much would get done. However, the majority of people I know could use a much healthier balance!

We can accomplish "rest" throughout our work days in many ways. Some ways will allow us to process our work more effectively, some will allow us to release the stress of our work, and some will motivate us mentally and physically to jump back into our work with a new perspective. When we do not take much-needed rest while working, we may become overwhelmed, tired, and dull. When we take physical and mental breaks, which suit our physical and emotional needs, we have the opportunity to bring new insight, new energy, and a new desire for our work.

Having a healthier balance throughout the day of work and rest also allows us to function with more positive energy when the workday is over and contributes to healthier relationships at home. When we finish our day with less stress and feelings of being overwhelmed, we have a better chance of having mindful conversations with our partner and children. We will have the energy needed to contribute to a family life which adds joy to the end of our days, rather than a drain on an already empty vessel.

Life today offers us minimal breaks if we allow it. It will consume us if we let it. When we consciously take control of our time and use it to better serve our mental and physical health we can see all it has to offer. We will see our friends for what they are; beautiful souls on their own path who we are as blessed to have us as we are to have them. We will see our partner for who they are: the person we choose to spend our hours, thoughts, dreams, and love with. We will see our children for who they are; young, impressionable minds looking for love and acceptance. We will see our boss for who they are: someone who gives us the opportunity to provide for our family, ourselves, and others we choose to help. We will see the haters in our lives for who they are: people who are projecting their own insecurities on us through judgment and hate. We will see that they deserve grace, just as we have received it in our lives. We will see the world around us for what it is: beauty, energy, and infinite possibility.

During my final year of teaching, I found I spent more time complaining, checking the clock, procrastinating, and pushing back necessary tasks more than ever. I was behind in my marking from the first assignment that crossed my desk in September to the final projects completed in June. I was getting through my days one 75-minute period at a time. I dreaded heading back to my classroom when the lunch bell rang. I found I needed to close my classroom door more often than I had in my eight years of teaching prior. I was tired of so many parts of my job. I didn't have to be doing them to be exhausted, I just had to think of doing them. I found my language around my job changed, my patience at home declined, and the quality of my work was at an all-time low. In this case, small mental breaks throughout my day were not going to be enough to revive me. I needed a large mental break from what had become a job rather than a passion.

Since following my heart out of the classroom, I have found it led me to the barn full-time. This was not my intention when I left teaching, but it felt so good. I still need small breaks, time to play with my daughter, quiet time to sit and drink a hot cup of tea, or time for a good conversation with a friend. I no longer crave breaks throughout my work day though. I do not look at the clock, telling myself I just have to get through 30 more minutes. I enjoy teaching again. I *want* to teach again, and I am learning that my enjoyment of teaching was separate from me being a classroom teacher. I have discovered that when you work at something aligned with your soul the balance starts to take care of itself. I know when I need to rest and take it easy because I know it will allow me to continue to love and live with empathy and compassion, both at work and at home.

I will continue to follow my heart and strive for balance in my life. This may be the only year my work is solely horse based. I may choose to focus more on my writing or I may find a new passion down the road. I am even open to returning to the education system someday if it is something that sparks a light in me. I have learned to never say never. So even though right now going back to a classroom seems a bit far-fetched, it may work again for me in the future. If at any point I begin to feel like I did in my final year of teaching, I must do some serious, conscious soul-searching and find work that fills me up rather than what tears me down.

We spend far too many hours a day working for it to be something we dread. Life is too precious to live feeling drained, worn-out, and beaten down. If this is how we are feeling we must tune into ourselves and discover what it is that is missing, find how to bring that into our lives more, and what we need to rid ourselves of to live happier healthier lives. Sometimes, it is just a matter of balance. Sometimes it is a life-changing discovery that turns your world on its head. Whatever it is, we are worth it.

Once we have successfully established how to create a healthy balance between work and rest in our personal lives, it is time to transfer the concept to our relationships as well. Anyone who has had a long-term relationship, whether romantic, business, or platonic, can tell you that relationships require work. Even the best of relationships need to be worked at or on. For the purpose of explanation here, I am going to use the example of marriage; however, the sentiment remains the same for all relationships.

No matter how well my husband and I are getting along, we still require a balance of work and rest. Rest is whatever we need to recharge ourselves to do our necessary daily tasks efficiently and happily. Our schedules are quite busy, and we spend a fair amount of time together due to the nature of our work, yet even when we are doing things separately, we are still working on our relationship.

Let me explain: My husband runs off lists. I should, but tend to not. I always say that his lists are *our* lists and my lists are *my* lists because his lists are so long it takes both of us to work through them successfully. When I am out grocery shopping and running errands, I am doing so in part to maintain a healthy relationship and functioning home. He relies on me to be able to accomplish certain things to free his time and mind to accomplish what he is doing and vice versa. We need to work together, yet separately, to function as a family unit. At the end of my day, I need a rest. I don't necessarily need a hot bubble bath. I need to turn off the to-dos and need-tos and just be. I have discovered that my "rest" in a relationship comes when I have time to feel connected to myself beyond my marriage. I require time to read a book I enjoy, shop with my sisters, or time with my husband doing non-marriage-maintenance stuff, like watching a movie, going for a ride, or taking our daughter camping. Personally, I think I need more rest than he does in our relationship, but this is part of the balance we discover when we are in tune with who we are, what we desire, and what we need.

In the past, I would consume myself with my relationship and lose sight of my true self and desires in the process. In my early twenties I left horses behind and took up golf following the interest of my boyfriend at the time, which was sort of fun, but it certainly did not light me up. In my mid-twenties, I moved to a city after a break up which really threw me for a loop. I didn't get thrown because I didn't expect the breakup. It was because I felt so disconnected from myself by the end that I would cry at the drop of a hat. Throughout the duration of the relationship, I had tried unsuccessfully to reconnect to myself by bringing horses back into my life, however, the relationship, our particular circumstance, and my priority in "self versus we" stopped me from getting what I needed out of my horses. My horses offered all the work and none of the therapy. I was frustrated by feeling like I was the only one who valued them, and as a result I felt like prioritizing them meant I was not prioritizing my relationship. My horses added stress to my life rather than help to release it, and my relationship suffered even more because of the resentment that built up as a result of my frustration, among other things of course.

Once I had ended the relationship, I found myself making choices I would have never made in the past. I couldn't quite figure out what was wrong; I just knew it wasn't right. When I was living in the city, I lived on the third floor of an apartment building. I remember standing at my bedroom window on one of the first beautiful days of spring and feeling lost. I needed to go outside and enjoy the day. I did not want to be restricted to walking to a shopping mall, or a walking trail or dog path. I needed a barn and chores to busy my body and calm my mind. In a desperate attempt to find something physical and outdoorsy other than riding a horse, I decided to take up running.

After a few weeks and dreading the whole process, from warming-up to attempting to climb the stairs to my apartment afterward, I stopped running. I have tried to revisit running a number of times over the years and have never got past the "I hate running" stage. I have never had an "I hate riding" moment, so I think I made the right choice to find my way out of the city and back into horses.

I did not walk away from horses due to a lack of love or passion, rather I walked away due to my desperation to fit into someone else's life; to amalgamate seamlessly. I lost sight of *me* in my pursuit to be *us*. I have learned through these experiences what having a relationship with someone who really loves me for me is all about. It is about maintaining all the pieces that make us who we are and creating a life with someone who embraces, encourages, and promotes each other's passions, dreams, and desires. I have discovered that I am able to maintain this through a balance of work and rest within my relationships.

I have spoken to so many women who confide in me that they have lost themselves in the shuffle of family life. They set aside their wants and needs for those of their children or husband. I have seen a pattern with women in their twenties. They search for the right man, find him, marry him, and have children.

Throughout the process, they acquire the titles of girlfriend, fiancée, wife, and mother. I often see these titles replace self. We are no longer an "I," we are a "we" and are supposed to be a team, remember? There is no "I" in "team" we are told! *Except, there is!* If we do not take care of our physical and mental health, our energy, our thoughts, and our actions, believe me, there won't be a team to worry about. Relationships take work and we simply cannot be our best self and certainly will not communicate our best if we do not have the right balance between work and rest.

In our newly, more balanced life of work and rest we will find it much easier to not only be present but feel and show appreciation for what we have in both our times of work and rest. We will have the opportunity to shift into gratitude for what is, rather than resentment for what is not. I have noticed personally that when I fall out of balance with work and rest, I feel anxious during my times of rest, and guilty and overwhelmed while working. My anxious feelings during rest happen due to my need to feel busy because there is so much to do that downtime feels wrong and unproductive. My guilt and feelings of being overwhelmed during work comes from my inability to do it all, and I begin feeling like I am failing at life. This is always a perfect indication for me that I need to slow down, certainly not to speed up, as my ego tells me I need to do. We cannot live in full gratitude and appreciation for what is when we are judging ourselves for things we have not done or still need to be done. We cannot be present and be consumed by the past and future at the same time.

Maintaining balance is something I still need to work on daily. Something I recommend everyone doing is consciously saying "yes" and "no." I am in the process of being more conscious of what is being presented to me, what I think of it, and if it is good for me. We need to be conscious to say yes to opportunities the universe gives us that add joy to our life, rather than limit ourselves by saying we don't have the time or can't for one reason or another. We have to listen to our heart. If we initially wanted to say yes and it gave us a bit of excitement, we should go for it! We attract what we want, but we are often so caught up in our thoughts that we miss opportunities and experiences that could bring value to our lives, even if the value is one good belly laugh, we deserve it. Say YES when you want, and then take care of the how.

On the other hand, saying NO is equally important yet so difficult for us people pleasers, especially when something does not light us up. Stop saying yes to things you do not like. If you are tired and resting in bed sounds more fulfilling than going to that birthday party, say no. You do not need to lie and come up with an elaborate excuse; your happiness is reason enough. Say no when you know you are only saying yes for someone else.

There may be some question here about tough situations like having to attend things we may not want to due to the circumstance, such as a friend's family member's funeral. This is an emotional situation many of us would like to avoid, but we must always think of the *why* behind what we do. We should say yes when we know our why is a direct result of love. If your friend says she needs your support in a time of loss, say yes, strengthen your connection and support them with your love. This will be good for you both.

If your friend calls and wants you to go to the bar with her in search of a booty call, that's another story, unless you feel like changing out of your pajamas because an adventure is exactly what you need to lift your spirits.

I think you get it. Say yes to more that makes you smile and brings joy to your life and say no to things that send you into an immediate negative headspace if they don't serve you on a higher level.

Just as our horses need time to rest to understand and appreciate what we are looking for when we are working them, we need to rest too. We need to use our time to reflect, recharge, and refocus.

Exercise:

Write a list of ways you can seek "rest" throughout your day (these may vary, but if you have a strong list you will have some that you can do anywhere):

Sample List:

-Take a walk   -Send an "I love you" to someone
-Listen to favorite podcast   -Meditate for 5 minutes
-Read   -Turn up the music
-Take a shower or bath   -Bake

-Write	-Watch a movie
-Call Mom	-Go for a drive
-Go to the gym	-Sit and play with the dog
-Take the kids to the park	-Go out for dinner
-Scroll through social media	-Hang out with a friend at home
-Grab a tea (drink in silence)	-Take a quick nap

Your List:

_____

_____

_____

_____

_____

_____

I encourage you to transfer this exercise into your journal. By getting into the habit of checking in every night, you will be more mindful of when you are falling off balance and can better determine how to achieve it again.

Date:_____

Today my work and rest balance was (circle one):

Perfect   Almost   Perfect   Slightly off Balance   Not Great   WAY OFF

Describe why you rated your day as you did:

_____

_____

_____

_____

_____

_____

Today I sought rest in the following ways:

_____

_____

_____

_____

_____

_____

_____

Tomorrow I will ensure that I balance work and rest by:

_____

_____

_____

_____

_____

_____

_____

CHAPTER TEN

Practice Makes Progress

*"The single biggest problem in communication
is the illusion that it has taken place."*

George Bernard Shaw

Throughout this book, we have looked at ways to communicate more clearly with ourselves and those around us. However, it truly all boils down to this one concept: When we are communicating, we must try to be as black and white as possible. When we eliminate gray communication from our lives our confidence in our decisions rise, our emotional state stabilizes, and our relationships flourish.

When we see people having a difficult time with their horses, 95% of the time their communication is gray. They are often asking initially with too much pressure and are not releasing at the right time or not at all, or they are asking for too many things at once, and both horse and handler become confused and frustrated. As a result, the horse either searches frantically for the correct response, gets annoyed with the pressure being inconsistently applied and not released, or they may respond in fear and use the reactive side of their brain because trust and respect have not been established.

In this chapter I am going to review the concepts we've covered and show how they establish black and white communication, resulting in us gaining confidence and happiness in ourselves, our relationships, and our lives.

When reading this, I don't want you to confuse "black and white" with rigid and non-flexible. Black and white communication is still soft and empathetic. Black and white communication is clear, conscious, and consistent.

Be Soft

Gray or unclear communication occurs when the communication does not fit the situation. Overreaction happens when we do not approach a situation mindfully; it happens to the best of us and is a hard habit to break. However, it in itself is the cause of many miscommunications and breakdowns in communication.

Our goal is to be genuinely and effectively soft. It is imperative that we are able to think with a rational mind rather than a reactive mind. Much like we teach our horses to do, we must be mindful to react with an empathetic response, connecting our response to the reaction of the person we are communicating with and the resulting situation. If we decide to only respond from a place of softness because we want to avoid conflict, we are not going to be genuine in our responses. People will sense a fake degree of kindness or may perceive us as someone they can take advantage of. Remember we can be soft in what we do but firm in how we do it. We have the ability to communicate with people in a way that builds both trust and respect.

Release Pressure and Reward Good Behavior

People do not change when they are met with combative energy. It creates tension and defensiveness that shuts down communication and growth. We focus on what others do wrong so often that we not only create a negative impact on them but we create a negative impact on ourselves as well. How we speak to and about others becomes a habit and translates to how we talk to and about ourselves. Negativity is habitual and destructive. We need to begin to focus our energy and communication on the things we see others do right in order to facilitate change in our relationships.

Remember "*I am going to let him sit and think about what he has done right.*" This can only occur when we are looking for what they are doing that is good, rather than only discussing what they have done wrong. We need to teach our children and ourselves that making mistakes in search of the right answer is going to bring pressure into our lives. However, when we approach life mindfully, we give ourselves the space we need to *find* the correct answer, let it *soak* in, and truly understand the feeling of success, self-confidence, and courage. Release the pressure on yourself and others and look to reward good behavior and you will find yourself shifting to a more positive and grateful mindset.

Respect is Not Transferable

We want people to respect us. This will not come if we are unable to set clear boundaries. We need to remember to take the time to think about our boundaries as we enter into new relationships. I know this sounds a little challenging, you may be thinking: *How will I know I don't like or approve of something if the person has not done it?* We won't be able to understand how we feel about every situation possible without experiencing the feelings that go with it. However, we certainly can imagine how we will feel for some everyday situations which present themselves. In particular relationship types, there are some things we do not have to experience to know they will be a no-go for us. Remember, we are responsible for communicating those things prior to them happening, during, or after for our boundaries to be set. If we never have the conversation, we are not setting the boundary. People are not mind-readers, and we need to make sure we keep our bodies and minds safe or no one else will. Be black and white. There is absolutely zero room for gray communication when you are setting clear boundaries.

Emotional State of Mind

We will be less frustrated with ourselves and everyone around us when we learn how we communicate and how we respond to other types of communication styles. We can use our new knowledge to engage in conversations that will foster relationships based on understanding. Learning our love languages and those of the closest people to us allows us to love people as they need to be. We do not need to only focus on this with our romantic partner; we should find out how our sister, mother, father, great-grandmother, and others naturally receive love. We can use it to aid in the growth of our relationships. We do not need to continually buy our sister gifts that she turns around and sells online when she really wants to sit for a cup of coffee with us and chat.

We should be sure to acknowledge when we feel frustrated in our lives. These are opportunities for education, empathetic conversations, and self-reflection.

This is Not For Me

This is one of the most important concepts in this book. I do, however, want to be clear on one thing. Do not let this line enable or feed your fears. When I found myself saying that specific horses were not for me I did not say they were never for me, just not right then. I have deliberately taken horses I would describe in this way to clinics to teach myself in a safe environment how these types of horses can be for me.

This being said, we must be clear with ourselves if something in our life is not serving us or is unhealthy. We must be kind enough to ourselves to let it go. Letting go of things that are not for us is a sign of strength, not weakness. Remember, only we can lift the weight off our shoulders. If we are strong enough to carry it, we are strong enough to set it down.

The Importance of Energy

With every passing day, my understanding of the importance of energy grows. We are energy; what our bodies are made of, what our thoughts produce, and how we communicate our intentions to the universe and everyone around us.

Surrounding ourselves with people, things, experiences, and habits that make us feel good is a must. We deserve to be happy. We cannot restrict ourselves from creating a life that brings us joy because we feel obligated to a specific person, job, or title. We need to be selfish with our energy. Take care of it, and it will take care of us. Remember finding the balance between work and rest to help restore our physical and mental energy will make us a better person and everyone around us will thank us for it.

Fear: The Quintessential Dream Crusher

The title says it all. You cannot set goals, chase dreams, or grow without the presence of fear. The key is to feel it and do it anyway. Understand that fear will present itself in a number of ways; anxiety, frustration, guilt, worry, anger, doubt, and more. We must be honest with ourselves when we feel these emotions and recognize that often we would not feel these things if there was no such thing as the opinion of others. If we had instant approval from everyone all the time, we would more than likely be running toward our dreams. Instead, we allow their voices to become our inner voice, and that keeps us from experiencing some pretty amazing things.

With every fear we conquer, our confidence will grow. Know that improving our confidence will not eliminate fear and thoughts of doubt, but we will have the ability to know that we are not our thoughts and our thoughts are not our reality. We will be able to shut down our own doubtful thoughts the same way we will learn to shut down conversations which will potentially leave us feeling drained from or guilty for.

Stepping Away from Drama

When we enter into drama we give away our own power. By succumbing to the drama of others, we allow negative thoughts to take hold and send us into a cycle of stress that is emotionally and physically unhealthy. We must be mindful of those who bring unnecessary drama into our lives and not take part in it.

We will have people enter into our lives who intentionally hurt us; this is the hardest sort of drama to remain disengaged from. The hurt will be real and will cause us to want to fight back. Fighting back will give us temporary relief, but it will not serve us in the long run. We cannot control the actions of others; we can only control our reaction to them. When we stay true to ourselves during these situations, we are able to approach the situation from a new and empathetic perspective. This allows us to see the true reasons why the other person is acting inappropriately, rudely, or in hurtful ways toward us.

It is important to remember that engaging in drama that attacks others, such as gossiping, is no less damaging to us. We need to shut down these conversations, or in the least, do our best not to participate and walk away. By not engaging in conversations that do not align with our values and morals we communicate clearly that we do not need to join in to feel like we are a part of something.

Sometimes our drama starts from within. We allow our thoughts to convince us we have more to worry about than we do or we convince ourselves that we are what we think. The challenging, but necessary, task is to be present enough to recognize when these thoughts take hold of us and to change our thinking at that moment.

Be black and white with yourself and others when it comes to drama. Be clear that you are not willing to enter into drama that steals joy. Maintain an empathetic mindful approach when discussing others, in and out of their presence. Possibly the most important thing to take from this is to be mindful of not entering into your own drama. Do not believe everything your mind tells you.

Balance Rest and Work

We cannot live a happy life without balance. To achieve balance, we have to make it happen. We have to know what makes us happy and lifts our spirits. It is vital that we prioritize our joy and say yes to positive opportunities and say a guilt-free no to things that do not add to our happiness. Our reward for working is rest, as it is with our horses. It is when we fail to offer our minds, bodies, and soul the rest they need that we become overwhelmed, frustrated, and unhappy.

Ensure that you are clear in your purpose while working and clear in your purpose while resting. Be present in your work to best relax when you need it. When we work while thinking of other things, such as arguments we had, the laundry we need to do at home, or the schedule for the kids this week, we do not dedicate our full selves to our work. This results in less productivity, prolonged tasks, and forced rest that feels like more of a burden than a blessing.

Exercise:

I encourage you to revisit each chapter as you need and complete each exercise as you feel necessary. Maintain a journal. Set aside time to think, write, and search within yourself. As you become more conscious of your communication, remember you will not be perfect all the time. Nonetheless, you will be better, and that is called growth.

BONUS LESSONS

"You are not working on the horse. You
are working on yourself."

Ray Hunt

Growing up with horses taught me some precious lessons. That is the reason, after all, that my parents invested in horses. They did not get a substantial monetary contribution at the end of their investment. Instead, they got well-rounded children who were taught values that have helped them become successful adults.

The lessons I learned from owning a horse at a young age are plentiful. I have selected the ones which I believe contributed the most to my success in life thus far.

If You Fall Off Get Back On

This can be perceived as a bit of a cliché lesson, but I am starting with it for a reason. It applies to a rider's first fall, in particular, no matter at what age it happens. Falling off your horse results in a number of painful experiences. Of course, there is physical pain, but aside from that, there is also the hurt ego, the shattered confidence, and often a touch of stinging embarrassment.

Physical pain is often the least difficult type of pain to push through. You see people push through physical pain all the time. People get tattoos, they get piercings, they take up boxing or martial arts, they play sports with sprains and breaks, and lots more. People will push through physical pain and find the pleasure on the other side. You do not, however, see people voluntarily experiencing emotional pain to gain pleasure.

We protect ourselves from emotional pain at all costs. We avoid situations that result in a hurt ego. We may not ask a person we like to dinner because they may say no. We avoid asking for a raise at work in case our employer does not see our value. We avoid the hard conversation with a significant other or refuse to apologize because that would be telling the ego it is wrong.

We seek situations to boost confidence and avoid ones that make us feel insecure. We get jobs we are more than qualified for to ensure we are the best. We take classes that are too easy to make sure we get top marks. We date people who love us more than we love them to avoid them hurting us. We leave relationships too soon to prevent the rejection we fear may come. We cheat on our lovers emotionally and physically because the other person feeds our ego and in turn, boosts our confidence.

We miss uplifting experiences due to the fear of embarrassment. We will stay seated when a person asks us to dance, robbing us of an experience worth having. We don't sing in the car like we want to in fear of someone seeing us. We avoid giving presentations for fear of making a mistake and having others notice. We don't go to the beach with the thought of others judging our weight. We fear what others will think and it stifles us.

When we are in situations that we know will result in emotional pain we procrastinate, we over-analyze, and we compromise all to lessen the blow. When the situation is unavoidable, such as divorcing an abusive partner, we will only make a move after much debate and deliberation.

People do not have to process nearly as much to push through physical pain, they see it as a means to an end, and they move toward the light on the other side. Emotional pain prevents people from seeing the good that will result from it, that is why we have such a difficult time pushing through it when we experience it.

With this, the question stands of why someone ever gets back on a horse after they fall. Combining physical pain with such emotional pain is a sure recipe for someone to give up or avoid that situation in the future, and it is for many. Not all though.

As a "horse person," I have heard countless stories from people who have said, "I rode a horse once but . . . " That sentence continues uniquely for most, but all of them end the same. It resulted in them never taking the chance again because of some combination of physical and emotional pain. Often, the individual did not even personally have the experience, they just have to hear of someone else's negative experience and chalk it up to it being not worth it, or too risky.

I am not entirely sure what sets apart the riders who get back on and push through their first fall and the riders who immediately give up and never grace a saddle again. I do know, however, that it takes great resilience to climb back on and this is something that will set them apart from others in the future.

As a former high school teacher, I see resilience on the decline. I see students giving up before they even get started. I see parents and teachers holding their hands for too long and never allowing them the opportunity to push through difficult situations independently. Those who learn to be resilient will rise above those who were never naturally inclined to or encouraged to be. We need people in this world who are willing to not only break through physical pain, but we also need people who are willing to push through the emotional pain that makes us question ourselves and the choices we make. It is crucial that we use these experiences to better ourselves and not allow them to write off life as too difficult and live in fear.

You Can and You Will

Confidence. This is the next lesson having a horse will teach you because as you push through the difficult times that make others walk away, your confidence grows. You learn that you can set goals and achieve them. You discover that learning something can be very challenging at first, you may fall, and you may feel awkward and unnatural at first, but before you know it when you sit in the saddle, it will feel as natural as walking. Your confidence will soar knowing that you can create a relationship with an animal built on trust and it will allow you to experience what it is like to fly without wings.

I often find myself saying to clients, "Fake it 'til you make it." A horse reads your body language and knows if you are not a confident leader. When this occurs, a horse will then feel as though they have to fend for themselves. They will be reactive and potentially dangerous. When we handle a horse with confidence, we become the leader of the herd, and they look to us to keep them safe.

This perception of an individual's confidence works the same way in our society. When someone walks into a room, we can sense their confidence, and it influences how we feel about their competency. This is a crucial thing to understand for those who are looking to succeed in all avenues they desire. We judge people based on their body language and their voice. It is natural to put our faith in those who present themselves in a confident way. I learned this in my teaching career where I saw individuals the same age as myself struggle to manage classes that gave me no trouble. In those first few years of teaching, I did not always feel confident, but I tried never to show it. I spoke clear and strong even when I felt my voice might break. I walked with my head high and shoulders back, even when my students towered over me. I handled situations as if I had dealt with them millions of times before, even in my first year. I faked my confidence about 50% of the time during the first couple years of teaching and with each successful lesson, class, semester, and year, my true confidence grew, and I very rarely had to fake it.

If students sense a lack of confidence, they will exploit it. If a potential client feels a lack of confidence, they will pass over us and work with someone who is "more experienced." If an audience perceives a lack of confidence, they will doubt our knowledge, talent, or ability and will feel uneasy as they watch us speak or perform. Confidence is key in moving forward. If we aren't confident in ourselves, others certainly won't be confident if us either.

I believe if we are living a life aligned with purpose we will always have to fake confidence from time to time. If we are breaking through fear and living outside of our comfort zone, we will encounter new situations that we will feel are scary and foreign that will require true and fake confidence to achieve success. We will always have firsts. Confidence is the very thing that will allow them from being a first to the first of many.

Good Things Come to Those Who Wait

Horses teach patience. Learning is a process, and we cannot teach our horses everything we want them to learn in a day. People who handle horses must appreciate the little breakthroughs and practice patience for the lessons to set in fully. If we rush our training, we will create problems down the road, and the same goes for ourselves. If we take shortcuts and do not have patience with ourselves, we will create bad habits that will interfere with our growth and success, or we will quit.

When we learn the skill of being patient, we feel less stress and pressure throughout life. Greatness and growth take time. When we learn patience, we understand that healthy relationships require our understanding and that we may have to wait for others to be what we need or give us what we need. We will handle our relationships with more care knowing that they do not have to be perfect every day. Things worth having take time and work.

We need to move beyond only wanting things in our lives that offer immediate gratification. In a world where we have the answers to all of our questions in our pocket, we must be willing to search beyond Google for answers; commit to relationships with people who do not text back immediately or do not share their feelings and life on social media. It is important to commit to developing relationships and friends based on invested time. This requires patience. We should allow the slow development of trust and love and allow connections between ourselves and others to grow based on experiences shared together. Like-mindedness is discovered through face-to-face conversation and comfort is found in quiet moments where neither person feels panicked to speak and fill the silence.

Good Things Come to Those Who Work

The skill of learning to wait has an equally important counterpart—the skill to work. Horses teach us that we have to work for what we have. We must put care into our work and appreciate the results. Everything about owning a horse is work. In time, people often find the work of cleaning stalls, grooming, and riding therapeutic, yet there are always days we have to go to the barn when we don't particularly want to. On cold, snowy days when buckets are frozen, and shoveling must be done it would be much easier to stay at home, but horses depend on us, and we need to work even when there is minimal payoff.

Growing up I questioned my commitment to my sport on more

than one occasion. I was envious of my friends who had fewer responsibilities and more free time. As an adult, I am thankful for my structured time and need to work hard. Due to my commitment to horses, I got into less trouble with alcohol and other things teens experiment with when they have unstructured time. When my friends were going to parties on Friday nights, I was going to Friday night lectures to learn how to feed, groom, and care for my horse to the best of my ability. I completed tests that I had to study for and competed in International Quizzes that required months of studying with only the reward of winning a ribbon and pride in knowing my hard work paid off.

Working hard is a skill. It is something we have to learn and practice. As adults, we have to press ourselves to work when it does not offer an immediate reward and sometimes no reward at all. The responsibility of owning an animal and belonging to a competitive sport taught me to "parent myself" at a younger age than some. I had a constructive self-dialog that pushed me to be responsible for doing things in life that I didn't feel like doing.

The first time I heard the term "parenting yourself" was when I was watching mentoring videos by Mel Robbins. I connected right away with this concept because it was something I had battled with throughout my teens and continue to do so as an adult. I have always been a goal setter and reaching goals took hard work and required the ability to parent myself through the times that I did not want to do something, knowing the inaction would hold me back from reaching my goals.

When people are not willing to work for what they have, they often find themselves stuck in a pattern where they are reacting to life rather than creating it. Those who do not work hard, blame others when things do not go their way instead of recognizing that with success comes failure and we are to learn from it and continue to work hard.

Be Present and Aware

With the integration of smartphones into our society so has the habit or practice of not being present and aware of what is happening around us. Working with horses taught me the importance of this at a young age, and it is reinforced every day. Horses live in the now; they do not think about the future, and are not envious of other horses, they simply live in the present moment and respond to their environment accordingly. If a handler is not present and aware when working with a horse, they are placing themselves in a potentially dangerous situation.

Being present and aware is a form of mindfulness that needs to be practiced when we have a tendency to feel like life is slipping away. When we are not present, we feel like we are no longer in the driver seat and this makes us feel a lack of control. When we find ourselves daydreaming, distracted, or dwelling on something, we are missing important moments in the present. We may miss the opportunity to speak with someone who could be the key to creating a much-needed shift in our lives, or we could miss the chance to boost our child's confidence by a simple "great job." Not being present could be as disastrous as running a red light and potentially taking a life or ending our own.

We must reconnect with our present to truly be happy in life. This means we need to appreciate what we have and to do that we have to be aware enough to see it. We need to beware of not clouding our judgment and perception of our own lives by looking at others and desiring what they have. If we find we are not happy it is our responsibility to be present in our lives and come to terms with our emotions. It is required that we take action, no matter how small, to create a present that we do not want to be distracted from.

Keep Moving Beyond Your Edge

Horses are brilliant, and they teach us as much as we teach them. When we are taught in our youth to set goals with our horse, it taught us to keep moving beyond our edge. We needed to make little steps outside of our comfort zone to learn something new and advance our skills. This is equally important as we progress into adulthood.

It is a common practice to leave school, choose a career path, and focus on our education to set us on our desired path. We choose our career path often between the ages of 16-25, and society tends to look down their nose at those who work within that chosen career for some time and then leave. Discovering the career path you chose as a teen or young adult no longer aligns with you, should not be something we frown upon. It is something we should encourage. We should promote personal growth and mental health. Feeling misaligned with your career path should be an indication that it is time to move forward, push beyond your edge, and create change.

Remaining in a job, relationship, city, or home that does not make you feel good is like saying you are not worth inconveniencing yourself to create your own happiness. We are responsible for moving forward in life. We are not required to settle for something because we thought it would be something we would enjoy down the road. This concept is ridiculous; it is like buying a gift for a friend we have not met yet; we do not know their likes or dislikes, and we do not know what has shaped them. Our future selves are very similar.

On the road of life, we are shaped by experiences, awakenings, and growth. We should expect changes in our desires and dreams. Only we have the ability to create change in our lives to chase those dreams.

It is here that I leave you with this: You have control over this amazing life. There is an abundance of knowledge out there to help you, and I encourage you to invest in it. Seek any opportunity that will bring light into your life, whether that be tea with a friend, a book, a hot bath, or a crazy adventure that takes you from coast to coast. Remember that if you do not approach your present with gratitude and see the good around you, you will never find the happiness you seek. You must appreciate the present to appreciate in the future. Find people who push you, not doubt you. When you think you are soft, soften more, you will find power in it, I promise. Lastly, thank you for joining me throughout this book. If you thought of someone that would benefit from any of my words, please pass it along, if you share it via social media use the hashtag #theconsciouscommunicator.

RECOMMENDED READING

For the recommended reading section, I choose to write the title and author solely, as many of these I have listened to on audiobook and also own the paperback, however, would not want to sway my reader either way. Some books may have more than one edition, and it is up to you as a reader to choose which suits your purpose best. My intention is to offer no more than five recommendations per chapter to make the list manageable for you. I encourage you to start with the ones that are recommended in correlation with the chapters which spoke most to you and only read those you believe will serve you. This is a personal list that I came across a number of ways, recommendations from friends or acquaintances or was drawn to at the bookstore. They came into my life when I needed them, as will the ones you are drawn to and decide to read.

Intention

The Untethered Soul by Michael A. Singer

The Power of Intention by Dr. Wayne Dyer

Stillness Speaks by Eckhart Tolle

The Wisdom of Sundays: Life-Changing Insights from Super Soul Conversation by Oprah Winfrey

Chapter One: Be Soft

The Compassionate Mind: A New Approach to Life's Challenges by Paul Gilbert

Daring Greatly: How the Courage to be Vulnerable Transforms the Way We Live, Love, Parent and Lead by Brené Brown

A New Earth: Awakening to Your Life's Purpose by Eckhart Tolle

Horses Never Lie by Mark Rashid

Chapter Two: Release Pressure and Reward Good Behavior

Resilient: How to Grow an Unshakable Core of Calm, Strength and Happiness by Rick Hanson, Ph. D.

Chapter Three: Respect is Not Transferable

The Power of Vulnerability: Teachings on Authenticity, Connection and Courage by Brené Brown

Chapter Four: Emotional State of Mind

High Octane Women: How Super Achievers Can Avoid Burnout by Sherrie Bourg Carter

Captivate: The Science of Succeeding with People by Vanessa Van Edwards

The 5 Love Languages: The Secrets to Love that Lasts by Gary Chapman

Chapter Five: This is Not For Me

The Power of No: Because One Little Word Can Bring Health, Abundance, and Happiness by Claudia Azula Altucher and James Altucher

The Highly Sensitive Person by Elaine N. Aron Ph. D.

Chapter Six: The Importance of Energy

Leveraging the Universe and Engaging the Magic by Mike Dooley

The Shift by Dr. Wayne Dyer

Ask and It Is Given, Volume 1: The Law of Attraction by Ester and Jerry Hicks

The Universe Has Your Back: Transform Fear to Faith by Gabrielle Bernstein

The Secret by Rhonda Byrne

Visit: sarahpeck.com

Chapter Seven: Fear: The Quintessential Dream Crusher

Big Magic: Creative Living Beyond Fear by Elizabeth Gilbert

The Gifts of Imperfection: Let Go of Who You Think You're Supposed to Be and Embrace Who You Are by Brené Brown

You are a Badass: How to Stop Doubting Your Greatness and Start Living an Awesome Life by Jen Sincero

The 5 Second Rule: Transform Your Life, Work, and Confidence with Everyday Courage by Mel Robbins

Girl, Wash Your Face: Stop Believing the Lies About Who You Are So You Can Become Who You Were Meant to Be by Rachel Hollis

Chapter Eight: Stepping Away From Drama

Girl Code: Unlocking the Secrets to Success, Sanity, and Happiness for the Female Entrepreneur by Cara Alwill Leyba

Judgment Detox: Release the Beliefs That Hold You Back From Living a Better Life by Gabrielle Bernstein

Braving the Wilderness: The Quest for True Belonging and the Courage to Stand Alone by Brené Brown

Chapter Nine: Balance Work and Rest

The Ripple Effect: Sleep Better, Eat Better, Move Better, Think Better by Greg Wells, Ph. D.

NOTES

My Intention

1   "The Sciences," Scientific America, <u>Gareth Cook</u>, October 22, 2013, "Why We Are Wired to Connect: Scientist Matthew Lieberman uncovers the neuroscience of human connections—and the broad implications for how we live our lives," <u>https://www.scientificamerican.com/article/why-we-are-wired-to-connect/</u>.

Chapter One: Be Soft

2   Liz Mineo, "Good genes are Nice, but joy is better," *Harvard Gazette*, April 11, 2017, <u>https://news.harvard.edu/gazette/story/2017/04/over-nearly-80-years-harvard-study-has-been-showing-how-to-live-a-healthy-and-happy-life/</u>.

3   Brené Brown, *Braving the Wilderness: The Quest for True Belonging and the Courage to Stand Alone* (New York: Random House, 2017), 39.

4   "SuperSoulConversations"OWNTV"BrenéBrown:WhattoDoWhenYouStruggle with Trust", accessed May 17, 2018, <u>http://www.oprah.com/own-supersoulsessions/brene-brown-what-to-do-when-you-struggle-with-trust#ixzz51TbhgA3S</u>.

5   "Home," Mindfulness Everyday, accessed May 20, 2017, <u>http://www.mindfulnesseveryday.org/</u>.

6   "Fitness with Lindsay," Facebook post, September 26, 2016, https://www.facebook.com/Fitnesswithlindsay/.

7   Find more information on Jim and Andrea Anderson of Higher Horsemanship at https://higherhorsemanship.com/.

8   Eckart Tolle, *A New Earth: Awakening to Your Life's Purpose* (New York, New York: Penguin Random House, 2016), 96.

9   "Buck Brannaman Quotes" Goodreads, accessed May 22, 2017, https://www.goodreads.com/author/quotes/16917.Buck_Brannaman.

Chapter Two: Release Pressure and Reward Good Behaviour

10 "About Automatic Thoughts," GET.gg, accessed May 23, 2017, https://www.getselfhelp.co.uk/thoughts.htm.

11 Brené Brown, *I thought it was just me (but it isn't): Making the Journey from "What Will People Think?" to "I Am Enough,* (New York, NY: Penguin Random House LLC), 199.

12 Ibid.

13 Brene Brown, *I thought it was just me (but it isn't): Making the Journey from "What Will People Think?" to "I Am Enough,* 242.

Chapter Three: Respect is Not Transferable

14 Vanessa Van Edwards, "Captivate: The Science of Succeeding with People," Penguin Audio, April 25, 2017, Audible.com.

15 "Society and Culture," Futurity, Posted by Gerry Everding-WUSTL, August 12, 2014, https://www.futurity.org/learning-students-teaching-741342/.

"The Protégé Effect: Why teaching someone else is the best way to learn," *TIME*, Annie Murphy Paul, November 30, 2011, http://ideas.time.com/2011/11/30/the-protege-effect/.

16 Northwest Association for Biomedical Research, accessed September, 26, 2018, https://www.nwabr.org/sites/default/files/ValuesActivities.pdf

Chapter Four: Emotional State of Mind

17 Marc Bekoff, *The Emotional Lives of Animals: A Leading Scientist Explores Animal Joy, Sorrow, and Empathy --- and Why They Matter* (Novato, California: New World Library, 2007), 9

18 Marc Bekoff, *The Emotional Lives of Animals: A Leading Scientist Explores Animal Joy, Sorrow, and Empathy --- and Why They Matter* (Novato, California: New World Library, 2007), 15

19 "Are We Talking the Same Language? How Communication Styles Can Affect Relationships: Figuring Out if You and Your Partner Are Speaking the Same Language," Psychology Today, Sherrie Bourg Carter Psy.D., Apr 27, 2011, https://www.psychologytoday.com/blog/high-octane-women/201104/are-we-talking-the-same-language-how-communication-styles-can-affect

20 Psychology Today, "Are We Talking the Same Language? How Communication Styles Can Affect Relationships: Figuring Out if You and Your Partner Are Speaking the Same Language."

21 Gary Chapman, *The 5 Love Languages: The Secret to Love That Lasts* (*Chicago*, IL: Northfield Publishing, 2015), 37.

22 Chapman, *The 5 Love Languages: The Secret to Love That Lasts*, 55.

23 Chapman, *The 5 Love Languages: The Secret to Love That Lasts*, 77.

24 Chapman, *The 5 Love Languages: The Secret to Love That Lasts*, 107.

Chapter Six: The Importance of Energy

25 Judy Christine Copp, "Your Energy System and The Law of Attraction," *A Higher Balance*, accessed June 2, 2017, http://ahigherbalance.com/writings-by-judy/your-energy-system-and-the-law-of-attraction/

26 Sarah Kathleen Peck, "The People Factor: It's All About Energy," *Accidental Creative*, accessed June 2, 2017, http://www.accidentalcreative.com/teams/people-factor/

27 Peck, "The People Factor: It's All About Energy."

28   Jill Blakeway, originally accessed on Pinterest, June 5, 2017, https://i.pinimg.
      com/564x/68/7f/d3/687fd32cc2c36b0f60fd7663bff73fa4--truth-quotes-
      karma-quotes-lies.jpg

Chapter Seven: Fear: The Quintessential Dream Crusher

29   Shelley M. White, "Mask your feelings, Mask Your Soul," *Collective-
      evolution*, accessed July 10, 2018, https://www.collective-evolution.
      com/2013/04/15/mask-your-feelings-mask-your-soul/

30   SuperSoul, Facebook post, December 17, 2015, https://www.facebook.com/
      SuperSoulSunday/posts/914180021962852

31   Mike Dooley, *Leveraging the Universe and engaging the Magic*, Simon &
      Schuster Audio, Feb 12, 2008, Audible.com

32   Mel Robbins, *The 5 Second Rule: Transform Your Life, Work, and Confidence
      with Everyday Courage*, Mel Robbins Productions Inc., February 22, 2017,
      Audible.com

Chapter Eight: Stepping Away From Drama

33   Hara Estroff Marano, "Depression Doing the Thinking: Take action right
      now to convert negative to positive thinking," *Psychology Today*, published
      July 1, 2001- last reviewed June 9, 2016, https://www.psychologytoday.com/
      ca/articles/200107/depression-doing-the-thinking

34   Marano, "Depression Doing the Thinking: Take action right now to convert
      negative to positive thinking."

35   Hara Estroff Marano, "Our Brain's Negative Bias: Why our brains are more
      highly attuned to negative news," *Psychology Today*, published June 20,
      2003- last reviewed June 9, 2016, https://www.psychologytoday.com/ca/
      articles/200306/our-brains-negative-bias

36   Marano, "Our Brain's Negative Bias: Why our brains are more highly attuned
      to negative news."

37 Marano, "Our Brain's Negative Bias: Why our brains are more highly attuned to negative news."

38 Soulful Equine® 195, accessed October 18, 2018 https://www.pinterest.ca/pin/38280665561638079/?lp=true

ACKNOWLEDGEMENTS

I would like to extend my deepest gratitude to anyone involved in making this publication possible. Your help, encouragement, and dedication to this book have made my dream come true. Writing this book has been life-altering. It was not easy, but at the same time, it was one of the most natural things I have ever committed to doing. I have been transformed by this experience, and I look forward to the adventures it takes me on. I am most looking forward to the conversations it initiates and the connections it creates and strengthens with like-minded people. However, in all honesty, I do not mind if this book only takes me to the local bookstore where I snap a quick photo of it on the wall collecting dust; it has given me all I need from it now. It has already created and strengthened connections and if this was all it was meant to do, well then it has been an incredible success.

I owe so much thanks to everyone who supported me throughout the process, from the blind faith of friends and family who had unwavering confidence in me, to the friends and family who are the "the proof is in the pudding" type and will be proud and supportive despite their skeptical nature. You have all helped me in your own ways along this journey.

A special thanks to Mike Porter, my loving husband who had no idea what he was in for when I first told him I was writing a book. Thank you for being there for me and believing in me when I was making decisions that most husbands would question. Thank you for seeing my need for change as *our* need for change and for showing me your love every day. Your role as a husband and father has come to you so naturally, and I am grateful for your energy, love, and understanding. You and Blake are my home.

I need to thank four ladies in particular for being the push and truth I needed on many occasions throughout the writing process. Lisa Martin, Kaelyn Woolaver, Nadine Smith, and Danique Henderson. You have all played a large role in bringing this to life. Each of you makes me a better person for knowing you and have impacted both the creation of this book and the person I am today. Thank you for your words of encouragement, your suggestions, and your friendship.

Thank you to both my mom and my mother-in-law. Mom, you have always believed in my "crazy" ideas and have shown me through example the true meaning of strength through softness when I needed you most. Teri, your love for our daughter has allowed Mike and I to live a life we are proud of. We could not do what we do without you. Mom and Teri, you have both made me a better person, and Blake is lucky to have you both to learn the value of love.

Vaughn and Dianne, thank you for your support and encouragement in all that Mike and I do. Our growth directly affected you, and we are blessed that you welcomed it with open arms and you continue push us further. I love that Blake is surrounded by family that shows her the importance of connection.

I need to acknowledge here my gratitude for all those who have contributed to my education and encouraged me to further my knowledge in all directions because no education is bad education. My biggest thanks here goes to my dad. The value you placed on my education has shaped me in many ways. I have always strived to make you proud, and when I see you, I can feel your love and pride. Your response to me many years ago in a brief email as I panicked about university, *Pressure makes diamonds,* still plays in my head when I feel the urge to quit. Thank you.

I cannot thank all of the educators enough who have taught me in schools, classrooms, staff rooms, homes, riding arenas, barns, and books. Your lessons have served me well and while you were trying to teach me one thing you inadvertently taught me many others and I am grateful. Your want to impart knowledge on others made me want to do the same. Your encouragement and example taught me how. I became an educator because of you, and I will always be an educator.

This thank you has to travel a long distance, but I know it will reach you. Papa, I feel you guide me when I am working with both horses and humans. I often ask you to take the reins when I see a student of mine getting into a bit of trouble. In my memory you are the epitome of soft and strong — must be where mom gets it. I can't wait to talk to you about all the special horses I have met along this journey because I know you are sending them.

A special thanks to Chelsea Thornton, my editor extraordinaire, your black and white personality was exactly what I needed for this project. I could not have selected a better person for the job. You brought my work to life.

I would like to express my gratitude to Balboa Press, a division of Hay House Publishing, for bringing this book to fruition.

Lastly, I want to say thank you to Elizabeth Gilbert for writing her book *Big Magic: Creative Living Beyond Fear* (Riverhead Books, 2015, page 429 and 430). I re-read this book as I was putting the finishing touches on my own and her words spoke to my soul. I read the following line on the very last day before handing this off to its final edit and these words repeated in my mind as I sent my work off: *"The final—and sometimes most difficult—act of creative trust is to put your work out there into the world once you have completed it. The trust that I'm talking about here is the fiercest trust of all."* She continued, *". . . fierce trust knows that the outcome does not matter."*

ABOUT THE AUTHOR

Photo Credit: Tanya Shields

Nikki Porter taught high school English and drama for nine years before focusing on her family, her writing, and her true desires. She and her husband run a small horse business, and she created East Coast Soul Sisters, a private Facebook group encouraging women to change their thoughts to change their life. She's also pursuing a career as a women's empowerment coach. Porter lives in Amherst, Nova Scotia, with her husband, Mike, and their daughter.

34019816R00148